"This is a great book! I can't imagine __ _____ _____ _____, _____, Christian, struggler—who wouldn't benefit from it. In fact, I'm sure almost anyone would be helped by this warm and intelligent apologetic for the Christian faith. I will recommend this book often, after first giving it to my own children."

Kevin DeYoung, Senior Pastor, Christ Covenant Church, Matthews, North Carolina; Assistant Professor of Systematic Theology, Reformed Theological Seminary, Charlotte

"Having sent four children off to large state schools for their college years, I am thankful that Michael Kruger has written this book. With compassion and clarity, he addresses key questions that often precipitate a crisis of faith for young believers. This accessible book equips families for good conversations about challenges to our faith, helping us trade panic and doubt for blessed assurance."

Jen Wilkin, Bible teacher; author, *Women of the Word*; *None Like Him*; and *In His Image*

"Every fall, untold thousands of young Christians step onto the college campus and are instantly engaged in the battle of ideas. They need help and encouragement, and Michael Kruger offers a wealth of both in this timely book. The help comes in his serious and faithful confrontation with the big questions that are unavoidable on campus. The encouragement comes from a wise author who is also a father and friend. The chapters are written as letters, and every college student you know needs every letter in this book. Where was this book when I went to college?"

R. Albert Mohler Jr., President and Centennial Professor of Christian Theology, The Southern Baptist Theological Seminary

"*Surviving Religion 101* is a crucial book for all Christians to read because the world that we inhabit has become the university culture of Michael Kruger's twenties. An epistolary book composed of letters from a loving Christian father to a faithful daughter entering the university, it invites us to ask crucial questions that help us make our calling and election sure. Are we intellectually prepared to understand and respond to the non-Christian thinking that surrounds us? If we believe that personal conversion and personal piety are enough for the Christian college student to survive, we are dangerously wrong. Our lack of intellectual preparation may explain why so many faithful Christians have had their faith shipwrecked by so-called progressive Christianity, living now with cultural change and social activism as proof of holiness. And for this reason, this book is as necessary for students entering Christian colleges as it is for those entering secular ones. Thanks be to God for this book. May it be used by God to preserve the faith of our college students and bring their unbelieving professors into the kingdom of God."

Rosaria Butterfield, Former Professor of English, Syracuse University; author, *The Gospel Comes with a House Key*

"The move from home to college and those influences that grip the mind from the age of eighteen to twenty-two play an absolutely decisive role in shaping the rest of our lives. The need for us to claim the Christian faith as our own at that point—and not as something we have merely absorbed from our parents or school friends—is exhilarating; but the process of so doing is often conflicted and intellectually, morally, and socially difficult. Michael Kruger is a well-known scholar, but he is also a parent with a vested interest in this issue and someone who himself experienced the range of challenges as a young student. In this clearly written book, he draws on all this to engage with the panoply of challenges that people face at college. While he covers the 'usual suspects'—the intellectual challenges to faith—what is so brilliant and helpful about this book is the way in which he understands and addresses the form of challenges to faith as they manifest themselves in today's therapeutic culture. Many students struggle with the claims of their faith because the moral tastes of our modern world make it seem so implausible. Kruger understands this and has written a book that speaks precisely to the kinds of problems that afflict college culture today. Students—and their parents—will find this work most helpful and enlightening."

Carl R. Trueman, Professor of Biblical and Religious Studies, Grove City College

"I wish I'd had a guide like Michael Kruger when I was in college. There's no one I trust more to help students navigate the difficult challenges to our faith that arise in both the classroom and also the dorm room."

Collin Hansen, Vice President for Content and Editor in Chief, The Gospel Coalition; Host, *Gospelbound* podcast

"Today's Christian students in secular universities face not just intellectual challenges to their faith. Perhaps even more caustic are the social and moral pressures. Michael Kruger ably addresses the intellectual issues, and as a high-powered Bible scholar, he is especially effective in dealing with the objections to God's word. But he also strengthens students for the more subtle spiritual trials they will encounter, addressing his readers with empathy and grace."

Gene Edward Veith Jr., author, *Loving God with All Your Mind* and *Post-Christian*

Surviving Religion 101

Surviving
Religion 101

Letters to a Christian Student on
Keeping the Faith in College

Michael J. Kruger

WHEATON, ILLINOIS

Surviving Religion 101: Letters to a Christian Student on Keeping the Faith in College
Copyright © 2021 by Michael J. Kruger
Published by Crossway
   1300 Crescent Street
   Wheaton, Illinois 60187

Cover image and design: Micah Lanier

First printing 2021

Printed in the United States of America

Unless otherwise indicated, Scripture quotations are from the ESV® Bible (The Holy Bible, English Standard Version®), copyright © 2001 by Crossway, a publishing ministry of Good News Publishers. Used by permission. All rights reserved.

Scripture quotations marked (NIV) are taken from the Holy Bible, New International Version®, NIV®. Copyright © 1973, 1978, 1984, 2011 by Biblica, Inc.™ Used by permission of Zondervan. All rights reserved worldwide. www.zondervan.com. The "NIV" and "New International Version" are trademarks registered in the United States Patent and Trademark Office by Biblica, Inc.™

All emphases in Scripture quotations have been added by the author.

Trade paperback ISBN: 978-1-4335-7207-4
ePub ISBN: 978-1-4335-7210-4
PDF ISBN: 978-1-4335-7208-1
Mobipocket ISBN: 978-1-4335-7209-8

Library of Congress Cataloging-in-Publication Data
Names: Kruger, Michael J., author. Title: Surviving religion 101 : letters to a Christian student on keeping the faith in college / Michael J. Kruger.
Description: Wheaton, Illinois : Crossway, [2021] | Includes bibliographical references and index.
Identifiers: LCCN 2020022288 (print) | LCCN 2020022289 (ebook) | ISBN 9781433572074 (trade paperback) | ISBN 9781433572098 (mobi) | ISBN 9781433572081 (pdf) | ISBN 9781433572104 (epub)
Subjects: LCSH: Christian college students—Religious life.
Classification: LCC BV4531.3 .K78 2021 (print) | LCC BV4531.3 (ebook) | DDC 248.8/34—dc23
LC record available at https://lccn.loc.gov/2020022288
LC ebook record available at https://lccn.loc.gov/2020022289

Crossway is a publishing ministry of Good News Publishers.

LB		32	31	30	29	28	27	26	25	24	23	22
15	14	13	12	11	10	9	8	7	6	5		

To Emma, John, and Kate,
May this book help you keep your lights shining brightly,
not only in college but for your entire life.
"Let your light shine before others, so that they may see your good
works and give glory to your Father who is in heaven."

Contents

Preface

Sometimes it seems that the book you are most eager to write is the book you never seem to find time to write. For many years now, such has been the case with the present volume. It has always been there, in a sense, in the back of my mind, just waiting patiently to be written. Every so often it would whisper to me, reminding me that it was there. But other projects took precedence, and the whispers grew more and more faint as time went along. Life happened, and soon the mental version of the present book entered a state of quiet hibernation in the recesses of my mind, probably wondering if it would ever be awakened.

Thankfully, through a number of circumstances, this book was awakened from its slumber. Perhaps not surprisingly, the primary reason for the reawakening was a life change relevant to its theme: my daughter Emma was accepted as a student at the University of North Carolina at Chapel Hill, the very place I had begun my own undergraduate studies exactly thirty years before. As I pondered her departure and the many complex and difficult challenges that awaited her, I remembered afresh my own university experience. As I explain in the introduction below, I was decidedly unprepared for what I would experience in college. And I wanted to make sure that she (and many other Christian college students) would not enter that experience unprepared. At that point, I knew this book *had* to be written. It was time.

But there was an additional reason that this book was stirred from its hibernation. My wife, Melissa, reminded me of its importance. For years, she had been gently prompting me to write my first lay-level book, and she was convinced that this needed to be the one. Sure, academic books were critically important too. But (most) college students were unlikely to read the ones I had written. They needed to hear from a biblical scholar but in a way that was more accessible to them. Given that she is both smarter and wiser than me, her voice is one I should have listened to long before now (along with the one inside my own head). But better late than never.

Now that this volume is complete, I realize that my own tardiness is perhaps part of a larger trend—and truthfully, a larger problem—within evangelicalism. The frequency with which Christian students head off to college and return (often in a short time) with a substantially different worldview than when they left should have occasioned some serious soul-searching within the evangelical church. Indeed, more than soul-searching, it should have occasioned a substantive response to address the problem. But it seems that such a response, except in a few isolated places, is largely yet to come.

As we wait, some profoundly important questions remain on the table. Why are our Christian college students not better prepared intellectually? Is it because, perhaps, our churches in general are not intellectually engaged with their faith? And is that due (at least in part) to having ministers who are also not thinking (and teaching) deeply about the Christian faith? And can that be traced back to the state of the average American seminary? I am sure there are many answers to these questions, and there isn't space to explore them here.

But there are, no doubt, many out there who think the church might need to awaken from its own slumber of sorts. Maybe the church is not asleep in terms of well-run programs or social activity or community engagement (though I am sure all these areas could be contested). But it might just be asleep intellectually. It might be time for a new doctrinal-theological-intellectual awakening in which the church recaptures her rich heritage of the Christian mind—and then considers various ways to pass that heritage down to the next generation.

Strange as it sounds, that means that this present volume is addressing a problem—adequately preparing the next generation to think deeply about its faith—that it cannot, in and of itself, fix. No one should be under the illusion, myself included, that this book will somehow keep Christian college students from deconverting. One solitary book, especially as introductory as this one is, could never address such a complex and multidimensional issue. Nor can it address every intellectual or theological need of the modern Christian college student. But I do hope it can help, at least a little bit. A nudge in the right direction, if you will. If even a solitary college student (somewhere) is helped, then I will count the labors to have been worth it.

Of course, the labors that made this volume possible are not all my own. Thanks are in order. Let me first thank Justin Taylor and the entire team at Crossway for their keen interest in this project. This is now my fourth book with them, and they are always a joy and delight to work with. A number of colleagues and friends have taken the time to read through these chapters (or at least some of them) and offer valuable feedback. In particular, I want to thank James Anderson, Crawford Stevener, Matt Howell, Ethan Brown, Julianna Mink, and Lindsey Harding. They provided many pieces of feedback, not all of which I accepted. So the blame for the final version lies entirely with me. The remaining shortcomings discovered by the reader (and there are many) probably just mean I should have done a better job listening to them!

Let me also acknowledge that a few small portions of the present material can be found in prior publications. Thanks go to Ligonier Ministries, the *Journal of the Evangelical Theological Society*, and the Gospel Coalition for allowing me to reuse this material. It should also be noted that a version of the section on genocide in chapter 14 was published in advance on my website, *Canon Fodder*.

I also want to thank my home church, Christ Covenant Church (PCA) in Matthews, North Carolina. It has been a joy being on staff there (part-time, of course) with my friend Kevin DeYoung. The large youth group there, along with Covenant Day School, has provided a great motivation for this book—it helps when you can actually see the faces of the people you are writing to. May they be the very ones who return home from college with their faith *stronger* than when they left.

Of course, a deep word of gratitude goes to Reformed Theological Seminary (RTS). It has been a profound joy to labor there these last twenty years. If we are to see a recapturing of the Christian mind in American evangelicalism, it surely will begin with seminaries. And on that score, I am convinced that RTS, by God's grace, is doing precisely what is needed to bring about that kind of change. May RTS continue to train men and women who have *both* a mind for truth and a heart for God.

The most profound thanks (at least on a human level) go to my family. My wife, Melissa, deserves tremendous thanks. Her wisdom, insight, and acumen—as both an editor and theologian—regularly amaze me. This book is better not only because of her input but also because she's my wife. I am a better writer, a better theologian, and especially a better person, because I am married to her.

But this book is written for my children, Emma, John, and Kate, three of the brightest lights in my life. Even if your lights flicker in college, may they never go out. And my prayer is that this book will help your light burn all the brighter, through college and for the rest of your life.

Introduction

In the fall of 1989, I began my freshman year at the University of North Carolina (UNC) at Chapel Hill. Like many freshmen, I was excited for the next chapter in my life, eager to explore the new opportunities and experiences that college had to offer. As the oldest state university in the country, and one with a strong academic reputation, UNC was a promising place for my new adventure.

Of course, I knew there would be challenges. College life would not be easy, especially for a Christian. But I had grown up in a solid Christian home, was taught the Bible from a young age, and was a faithful member of my church youth group. And there had been no shortage of advice about my forthcoming college experience—from parents, older friends, and even my youth pastor—all keen to offer warnings about the dangers and pitfalls that awaited me. So I figured I was ready.

I wasn't.

Now, it's not as if I was entirely unprepared. When it came to moral issues (substance abuse, sex, and the party scene) and practical issues (how to get along with my roommate, manage my budget, and stay focused on my studies), I had received plenty of good input. And to be sure, these are important things for any college student to address. Many believers have shipwrecked their faith over such matters.

The problem stemmed not from what I was taught but from

what I wasn't taught. I wasn't prepared in the one area that would matter most in a university environment. I wasn't prepared *intellectually*. And I would soon learn (the hard way) that intellectual preparation was what I needed more than anything.

Of course, in retrospect, it seems a little surprising that I wasn't more intellectually prepared. After all, I was headed to a big university where foundational academic issues would surely arise. So why wasn't I ready? I am sure there were a number of reasons. Although I was a good student in high school, my free time wasn't spent studying Greco-Roman religions or biblical archaeology. Like any teenager, playing sports and hanging out with my friends occupied most of my time.

But my lack of preparation wasn't just because I was a teenager. The Christian culture in which I grew up also played a role. The most important issues in the evangelical world of my youth were *personal conversion* (was I saved?) and *personal piety* (did I live like a Christian?). To be clear, I think these two issues are very important, and I am tremendously grateful to have grown up in churches that did not ignore them (in our current day, many churches need a renewed focus on them). But generally speaking, my theological training stopped there. There was very limited instruction on the Christian worldview—what we believe and why we believe it—and virtually no instruction on how to respond to non-Christian thinking.

In short, I learned to love God with my heart but not with my mind. There was no category (or at least a very limited one) for an intellectual expression of my faith that was rigorous, deep, and well reasoned.

Needless to say, I don't believe my experience as a youth was unique—either back in my day or in the present. While evangelicalism is certainly not monolithic, most would agree that large segments of the movement today still lack deep doctrinal reflection and intellectual engagement. That could be due to a focus on personal piety and conversion (as in my youth experience), or it could be due to evangelicalism's newer fascination with social action and cultural change. Either way, the development of the Christian mind has not been a priority. Surely, therefore, many Christian college students over the years have found themselves in a position very similar to my own—lots of zeal but little knowledge. Indeed, that reality is part of the motivation for writing this book.

My lack of preparation reached a head in the spring of my freshman year when I took a religion course titled Introduction to the New Testament. The professor was a young scholar who was bright, engaging, funny, and persuasive. It didn't take long to see that he lectured with an eye toward evangelicals, even sharing how he was once an evangelical himself not long ago. He used to believe what we believe, he told us. He used to think like we did. And then during his graduate studies, after deep engagement with the text, he realized he could no longer maintain his evangelical beliefs. The New Testament wasn't inspired after all but was full of mistakes. It wasn't reliable but was filled with made-up stories and fabrications. And its original form wasn't even accessible to us but had been badly corrupted by scribes over years of transmission.

In short, argued my professor, the historical evangelical position on the Bible is intellectually untenable. It is a book not from God but from men. You can believe it with your heart—after all, isn't that what religious people do?—but you cannot (or at least should not) believe it with your mind.

That professor's name was Bart Ehrman.

Although I could not have known it at the time, I was taking a class with a scholar who would become one of Christianity's

In short, the universities are doing these Christian students a favor.

On the surface, all that sounds eminently reasonable. Who's not for intellectual freedom? The question, however, is whether modern universities are actually exhibiting the intellectual freedom they claim to value. Are they genuinely interested in presenting both sides of the argument? As one sample area, consider the way modern universities represent political views. A recent article by Cass Sunstein, professor at Harvard Law School, highlights the fact that professors at the top major universities are overwhelmingly Democrat in terms of political affiliation, vastly outnumbering Republicans.[2] At some of the most liberal colleges and universities (e.g., Wellesley, Swarthmore, Williams), this ratio was a mind-blowing 120 to 1. Sunstein, a Democrat himself, laments this fact, calling it "genuinely disturbing." He states, "Students are less likely to get a good education, and faculty members are likely to learn less from one another, if there is a prevailing political orthodoxy. Students and faculty might end up in a kind of information cocoon."[3]

Now, this present volume is not about politics, nor am I picking sides in the Democrat versus Republican debate. I mention these statistics on political affiliation only to illustrate a simple point: university students are not, generally speaking, hearing both sides of arguments. It seems that modern universities are for every sort of diversity (gender, race, ethnicity) except diversity of ideas. And nowhere is this trend more evident than in religion classes. Sunstein points out that when it comes to individual academic departments, religion faculties have some of the most lopsided ratios of liberals to conservatives, exceeding 70 to 1.

Indeed, as noted above, my Introduction to the New Testament class was decidedly one-sided. If my own upbringing was religious indoctrination, then one might argue that this class was just another form of religious indoctrination—only in the opposite direction. The class was not so much a rejection of absolutism as the mere exchange of one set of absolute beliefs for another.

Needless to say, it is difficult for the average nineteen-year-old freshman to recognize that this is what is happening in his or her university class. Students often see the clash before them as one between religion and science. On the one side are those dogmatic, biased religious folk, conditioned (even blinded) by their faith commitments. On the other side are neutral, unbiased, open-minded historians—trained in the finest universities in the world—who are merely giving you the "facts." Given that framework, it is not hard to imagine why most students respond the way they do.

Unfortunately, the ideological state of the modern university is unlikely to change anytime soon. In the meantime, Christians need to think more seriously about how to prepare the next generation of believers to handle the intellectual challenges of the university environment (and beyond). We need to do more than prepare them morally and practically; we need to train their minds to engage effectively with an unbelieving world.

So how's that going to happen? Ultimately, it will require a macro-shift in the broader evangelical world, moving beyond just pietism and revivalism and recapturing the deep historical and intellectual roots of the Christian faith. And then, that same evangelical world must think carefully and critically about how we pass that robust version of the faith to the next generation. Admittedly, that sounds like an overwhelming challenge. But we can take baby steps in that direction. This book is designed to be one of those baby steps.

While there are already numerous books that offer practical guidance and advice to Christian college students, very few directly engage the intellectual minefield they face. Today's college students need more than dating advice and tips on how to make good grades. They need a framework for dealing with the flood—no, tsunami—of intellectual attacks they will receive from their professors, classmates, and campus organizations. Sure, Christians outside college face similar challenges from our culture. But the intensity and concentration of these challenges in a university environment is unmatched. And college students are dealing with these immense pressures at a relatively young age. That's why the intellectual preparation of Christian students for college must be a priority.

This present volume is designed to help in that preparation by tackling not only the key issues in biblical scholarship but also the flashpoints of our cultural conversations in a manner that is accessible to college students (and, hopefully, even seniors in high school). My desire is that *Surviving Religion 101* provides an intellectual pathway for Christian students so that they can keep their faith without sacrificing their intellectual integrity.

As indicated above, this issue is personal to me because of what I experienced as a college student. But it is also personal for another reason. In 2019, my daughter Emma left for college. And where did she go? The University of North Carolina at Chapel Hill. So exactly thirty years after I went to UNC, it seems things have come full circle. Who knows, maybe she'll even have Ehrman as a professor. Although she has already left for college, I have written this book for her and for my other two children, John and Kate, who will soon follow. My hope is that it helps them realize that belief in Christianity is not just intellectually defensible but also intellectually *satisfying* at the deepest of levels. Yes, we believe God with our hearts. But we can also enjoy him with our minds.

Because my daughter Emma is now in college, I have structured each chapter as a "letter" to her. And each letter will answer a question (or series of questions) that I know she will face. Such a format is designed to keep the book both personal and accessible—rather than an unceremonious dumping of facts on the unsuspecting reader, bolstered by a sea of footnotes. I am not writing for scholars, nor even for skeptics. I am writing for students.

Of course, I am not under the impression that merely reading this book will answer every possible question a college student may have. Nor do I think any single book (or even many books) could prepare students to go toe-to-toe with their college professor. No, the intent here is much more modest. Like any complex task, eventually you have to take the first step, even if it's a little one. This volume is designed to be that first step, an initial orientation for Christian students about the challenges they face and (hopefully) a reason for them to be confident that there are answers to their questions, even if they don't yet have them.

Or as the title suggests, this book is about *surviving*—with faith intact—one's university experience. Now, that may seem like a strange goal, perhaps one that is far too modest. Don't we, as Christians, want to do *more* than survive? Don't we want to make an impact and change the world while in college? Sure, but that's not where one starts. Instead, you start by not stopping. By not giving up. By surviving. You can't "change the world" for Christ if you no longer believe in Christ or walk with Christ.

So let us turn now to the challenges in the "letters" that follow. My prayer is that these are an encouragement to my daughter Emma, to John and Kate, and to the many other college students who read them in the years to come.

I'm Worried about Being a Christian at a Secular University— How Will I Survive?

To say that college does something to the average student's religion is to state a truth which will be conceded by anyone who has given the matter a moment's thought.
PHILIP WENTWORTH, *THE ATLANTIC*, 1932

Dearest Emma,

Move-in day was really tough. And I don't just mean hauling all your stuff up five flights of stairs to your dorm room! It seems like only yesterday that I held you in my arms as a newborn baby and welcomed you into the world. I can still remember leaving the hospital and thinking to myself, *Do we just get to take her home? Aren't there instructions on how to do this?* And now, eighteen years later, you are all grown up and on your own. As we drove away from the campus, I thought to myself, *Do we just leave her there? Aren't there instructions on how to do this?* Mom and I shed many tears that day.

I know that move-in day was also hard for you. On the drive to Chapel Hill, I could see your anxiety growing with each passing mile. And that's understandable. Going to college is a big transition with much to worry about: making friends, fitting in, picking a major, keeping up your grades. Plus, you will be doing all this on your own—without anyone looking over your shoulder. It all seems so new and strange.

But most of all, I know that you are wondering what it will be like as a Christian at a big secular university. You are not naive about the way our modern world views your faith. And you know that what you believe will be challenged (even ridiculed) in profound ways by both professors and students. On top of this, you have already seen older Christian friends who have gone off to college and have begun to waver in what they believe. Some have even abandoned their faith entirely.

These sorts of concerns are bound to produce some angst in any first-year student. So what can you do to survive this crazy new world of college? Here are some initial thoughts for you as you begin your new life away from home.

It's a Dangerous Business

As you think about the challenges of college life, you may begin to wonder whether this whole issue is a bit overblown. Aren't we being a little alarmist when we paint college as this "dangerous" place for Christians? Aren't we just scaring parents with exaggerated stories about how big, evil universities will devour their children? Don't many Christians have a wonderful college experience and leave with their faith fully intact? And aren't some faculty members themselves committed Christians?

Absolutely! There's a sense in which the answer to all these questions is yes. I don't want you to enter college with an overly pessimistic view of your situation, convinced that everyone is out to get you and paralyzed by a martyr complex. Like the group of kids in the movie *The Sandlot* (which you loved as a child), sometimes we can create monsters that aren't really there. In their minds, behind their baseball field, the junkyard dog—which they called "The Beast"—was six feet tall, roared like a lion, and shook the ground when he walked. It's only at the end of the film, when they meet him face-to-face, that they realize they've had overactive imaginations. He's just an ordinary dog after all.

So we need to be careful not to see monsters around every corner. Please know that your non-Christian professors are not Darth Vader, and your fellow students are not part of the Inquisition looking for evangelical Protestants to string up.

At the same time, we must also guard against the opposite mistake. If unbridled suspicion is a problem on the one side, then a naive overconfidence may be a problem on the other. Some young Christians enter college absolutely convinced that nothing can shake their faith—they are mature enough, wise enough, and theologically astute enough to handle whatever comes their way (so they think). There's nothing to worry about, they tell themselves. Falling away is always something that happens to *other* people.

But this is precisely the kind of thinking you need to avoid, Emma. It both underestimates the real pitfalls of the university environment and overestimates your own strength and ability. As for the pitfalls, don't minimize them. Serious intellectual challenges are coming your way—arguments you've never heard, facts you didn't know, issues you've never considered. Beyond this, such challenges are being delivered by professors who are bright, persuasive, compelling, and eminently likable. Even more, you will hear these challenges repeated over and over (sometimes to the point of exhaustion) by your fellow students. And if you don't change your views, you might be regarded as narrow minded, intolerant, arrogant, and even hateful.

So are you ready for that? I suppose most eighteen-year-olds are not. And as mature as you are, Emma, you, too, need to recognize your own weaknesses and vulnerabilities. In principle, *all of us* are susceptible to falling away. That's why the Bible repeatedly warns us that we must persevere to the end. We must keep running the race and not give up.

When you were much younger, I used to read *The Lord of the Rings* aloud to you and John and Kate. The three of you sat together, listening to every word. You might remember that in *The Fellowship of the Ring*, Frodo was a young hobbit always eager to go on adventures with his uncle Bilbo. But Frodo recalls Bilbo's wise advice to him about such adventures. Yes, there are beautiful mountains and wonderful treasures. But there are also real dangers and frightening enemies: "It's a dangerous business, Frodo, going out your door. . . . You step into the Road, and if you don't keep your feet, there's no knowing where you might be swept off to."[1]

So what does all this mean? It means that as you head off to college as a believer, you need to realize that it can be "a dangerous business." Don't take your spiritual health lightly while you're there. You need to be serious about the potential challenges you will face, while at the same time not living in fear and worry. Simply put, "Be on your guard" (1 Cor. 16:13 NIV).

Of Course You Don't Have All the Answers!

As you jump into the intellectual fray at UNC, it will quickly become clear that there are many questions you don't know how to answer. Maybe it will be questions about God (If God is good, then why is there so much evil in the world?) or questions about the Bible (How can you believe in inspiration if there are contradictions in the Gospel accounts?) or even questions about science (Hasn't genetics proved that the human race did not originate with just two people?).

Whatever the question might be, it can be very uncomfortable not having an answer. The intellectual give-and-take of a big university environment can be intimidating. If you get caught on the losing end of an exchange with your professor or classmates (whatever that may mean), you might feel silly or embarrassed. It might make you withdraw from future conversations or even lead you to doubt what you believe.

But should your lack of answers lead to this sort of reaction? Not at all. First, you need to give yourself a break. Most eighteen-year-old Christians are not fully equipped to answer the barrage of complex (and aggressive) questions coming their way, nor is it reasonable to expect them to be. What first-year student is able to go toe-to-toe with a professor? Of course you won't have answers to every question! Why would you ever think you should or could? Don't hold yourself to an unrealistic standard.

Second, not having an answer does not affect the truth of what you believe. Your beliefs can be absolutely correct, even if you cannot explain or defend them. Consider other beliefs you might hold. If asked whether you believe humans landed on the moon in 1969, I imagine you would say you do. But if you happened to strike up a conversation with a moon-landing denier (these folks are more common than you think) who shared all his well-crafted objections and pressed you to defend your beliefs, you would probably have very few answers. But surely you wouldn't abandon that belief just because you were stumped. Your belief would still be correct.

The fact is that most things we believe are like this. We haven't had time to *personally investigate* each and every belief we hold—instead, we rely on other authorities. A person might believe that E=mc², that Constantine won the Battle of Milvian Bridge, and that her grandfather was born in George, Iowa. But few could defend these beliefs on the spot if pressed by a determined critic who was eager to question everything.

Third, don't confuse not having an answer with there not being an answer. The two are not the same. Even if *you* don't have answers to difficult questions, that does not mean there are none. Indeed, you should know that most of the objections you will hear are old news (even though they are often presented as if no one had ever thought of them before). A little research will show that Christians have been wrestling with these issues—and offering coherent answers to these issues—for generations. In fact, some of these objections were answered in the first few centuries of the early Christian movement. Moreover, there are many Christian scholars out there who have provided comprehensive answers to these questions (though secular professors often refuse to discuss those arguments).

Here's the big point: you're not going to be able to answer every objection to Christianity that you hear. And that's okay. You just need to be ready for that. It's not a reason to doubt your faith.

What Doesn't Kill You Makes You Stronger

As hard as it is to endure severe opposition to what you believe, there is an upside. To quote Kelly Clarkson, "What doesn't kill you makes you stronger" (though, as a side note, this was originally said by Friedrich Nietzsche). What does this mean? It means opposition can actually be a blessing. As with a weight lifter or professional athlete, the pain of resistance can actually create more strength and endurance.

Think back for a moment to your soccer-playing days. It was the end of practice that was always the most miserable because your coach would make you run "suicides"—a near-endless amount of sprinting back and forth across the field until your lungs were on fire and you felt like throwing up. At first glance, the whole scene seems sadistic. It might look as if your coach were out to destroy you. After all, he was inflicting severe pain on you! But as a player, you knew better. You knew your coach was just preparing you for the state tournament at the end of the season, when every last drop of endurance would be needed.

In a similar way, the opposition you endure at UNC can, as strange as it sounds, be a tremendous benefit. It can shape you into a better, fitter believer who can serve God in unique and exceptional ways—ways that would be impossible in an opposition-free life.

For one, opposition will force you to sharpen your thinking. It will force you to find the answers to the tough questions. It will push you to be a better theologian. Truth be told, most Christians are never really required to do this. We live most of our lives in a Christian bubble, surrounded by Christian friends in our Christian subculture. It's very peaceful and comfortable. But comfort never produces good soldiers. And that's what we are called to be. Paul said, "Share in suffering as a good *soldier* of Christ Jesus" (2 Tim. 2:3).

I found this to be true in my own experience at UNC. As I've told you before, I had Bart Ehrman as a professor when I was a freshman. I didn't know it at the time, but I was taking a New Testament class with a professor who would become one of the leading, and most vocal, critics of Christianity, authoring over thirty books. It was a painful experience for me as I heard attack after attack on what I believed.

But God used it to strengthen me. The opposition didn't make me quit (by God's grace) but instead made me pursue my faith with more vigor. I sought out the answers to my questions. I chased down the resources that could help me respond to Ehrman's claims. I read everything I could get my hands on about the origins of the New Testament. In many ways, it was a means of survival. I didn't want to end up like so many others who abandoned their faith.

Let this be true of you, Emma. Let all these questions drive you to pursue the answers. Be a reader. Be a studier. Be someone who dives into the deep issues of your faith. And here's the payoff: not only will that bless your own soul, but it will bless many, many other people as you help them work through challenging intellectual issues. You can become a resource for others.

The Christians in the earliest generations of the church also learned this lesson. In the second century in particular, Christians faced an unprecedented barrage of attacks. Some of those attacks came from the intellectual elites of the Greco-Roman world, heaping scorn and ridicule on the burgeoning Christian movement. In their eyes, Christianity was intellectually lacking and philosophically deficient, attracting only the uneducated and gullible (especially, they argued, women and children).

But attacks also came from within. Numerous heretical groups arose, questioning foundational doctrines of Christianity and amassing an impressive number of followers. In particular, Gnosticism was a serious threat. The Gnostics argued that the physical world was the creation of a false god and that Jesus, therefore, could not have really come in the flesh. Moreover, they argued that "salvation" came not through the work of Christ on the cross but through a special knowledge given to only certain enlightened ones.

Such challenges—from both inside and outside—created a bit of a crisis in the early Christian movement. How would they respond? Would the infant church even survive? And here we see again that God uses challenges and opposition for good ends. Not only did the early church survive, it thrived. How? It dug deep and pursued these tough theological and intellectual questions. The earliest Christian leaders learned how to express their faith in better ways, clearer ways—ways that would distinguish it from (and would refute) the various heretical groups around them.

In short, opposition made early Christians better theologians, better defenders of the faith, and better evangelists. Such theological reflection and nuance culminated in the beautiful and unmatchable Nicene Creed of AD 325, where the church expressed its commitment to Christ as both God and man united in one person, over against opposing views.

But opposition to your faith will change you in another way. In addition to sharpening your mind, it will also hone your character. It will force you to trust the Lord in new and even radical ways—to lean on him and not your own understanding. It will give you a patient spirit and calmness under pressure. And most of all, it ought to give you love, compassion, and sympathy for those who don't know Christ.

Here's the big point: don't view opposition only in negative terms; view it as an *opportunity* to grow as a Christian, so that you might be better equipped to build up your fellow believers and reach non-Christians more effectively.

Band of Brothers (or Sisters!)

I can still remember the first time I saw the World War II film *Saving Private Ryan*. The opening scene of the D-Day invasion was so profoundly gut-wrenching, I almost had to leave the theater. It's the first time I think I ever really got a taste (just a taste, mind you) of the horrors of war. I could barely watch as those brave US soldiers stormed the beaches of Normandy, knowing it was almost certain they would die. And at Omaha Beach, most of them did. The Nazis were dug in at elevated positions, forcing the Americans to charge forward, unprotected on the open beach, into a barrage of bullets and explosions.

When faced with such incredible heroism, an obvious question comes up. What enabled these soldiers to be so brave? What could explain a person's willingness to give his life so courageously?

I suppose there are many answers to those questions. But as the movie wore on, one answer became quite clear. After the Normandy invasion, the movie tracks a small band of soldiers who take a harrowing journey through war-torn France to find a solitary soldier, Private Ryan, and bring him home. Ryan had lost his three brothers, and the State Department didn't want his mother to lose her fourth, and last, son.

After Private Ryan is finally found, it turns out he doesn't want to leave. He wants to stay and fight. And here's why: "You can tell [my mother] that when you found me, I was with the only brothers I had left. And that there was no way I was deserting them. I think she'd understand that."

Here's the answer (or at least one of the answers) for how soldiers could exhibit such unimaginable bravery: *they didn't do it alone.* For Private Ryan, it was the camaraderie, the brotherhood, the friendship—centered on a common goal—that made him so willing to give his life. And the same could be said of the countless soldiers who died on Omaha Beach. They could do things together that they could never (and would never) do apart. They were a band of brothers.

The same is true of the Christian life, Emma. You are not headed to the beaches of Normandy, of course. But the Christian life is a battle, and you are one of its soldiers. And the university environment can be a hot war zone with lots of enemy fire. So how do you survive it? Don't go it alone. You've got to find a band of brothers and sisters to walk together with you.

First and foremost, that involves finding a good local church. You need a church home where you can be a member, get involved, and sit under the preaching and teaching of the word of God. There are lots of church options, but make sure to find one that believes in the gospel message—we are saved by grace alone through faith in Christ alone—and that affirms the inspiration and authority of Scripture.

Similarly, you need to find a good campus ministry to plug into. This won't replace the local church, but it will be a vital part of your on-campus life and fellowship. Here's where you can meet fellow believers who can walk with you through the ups and downs of college life. Their encouragement can keep you going, especially when things are difficult. As the book of Hebrews says,

> And let us consider how to stir up one another to love and good works, *not neglecting to meet together*, as is the habit of some, but encouraging one another, and all the more as you see the Day drawing near. (Heb. 10:24–25)

And here's what you have to look forward to. Many of those friends—your band of brothers and sisters in college—will be dear friends for the rest of your life. Some of the strongest bonds are formed in the field of battle. They are a blessing not just for four years but maybe for forty years!

———

Emma, we are so excited to see you head off to college. I know it's a time of great anticipation and fear mixed together. But I know you are ready. You are on your guard because you know, as Bilbo said, that the college adventure can be "a dangerous business." Don't panic when you don't have the answers—they're out there even if you don't yet have them. And most of all, stick with your band of friends who can spur you on to love and good deeds.

Our prayer is for you to stay faithful not only in college but throughout your whole life, so that you can say with Paul, "I have fought the good fight, I have finished the race, I have kept the faith" (2 Tim. 4:7).

Love,

Dad

My Professors Are Really Smart— Isn't It More Likely That They're Right and I'm Wrong?

What you see and what you hear depends a
great deal on where you are standing. It also
depends on what sort of person you are.

C. S. LEWIS, *THE MAGICIAN'S NEPHEW*

Dearest Emma,

By now, I imagine you are feeling very alone. It's strange, isn't it? Even though you're on a big campus surrounded by nearly twenty thousand students, it is still easy to feel isolated. This can be true socially but also (and perhaps especially) true intellectually and theologically. What you believe—about God, Jesus, the Bible, salvation—makes you a pretty rare creature. Yes, there are others like you in your Christian fellowship, but your group makes up only a tiny percentage of the campus.

Right now, I know that you are pushing through this feeling. And I'm proud of you for standing firm. But over time, the intellectual loneliness takes its toll. Your classmates will look at you like you're weird, your suite mates will wonder why you have such intolerant beliefs, and your professors will view you as one who needs to be deprogrammed from your religious upbringing. It's hard feeling like the odd one out.

Most fundamentally, this feeling will begin to raise deep and important questions in your mind: If Christianity is true, then why don't more people believe it? And why does it seem like the smartest people around are precisely the ones who don't believe? If Christianity was *really* true, if Christianity *really* made the most sense of the world, then wouldn't most people accept it?

These questions will be particularly acute when it comes to your professors. There they are, trained in some of the finest research universities in the world. Brilliant. Smart. Filled with knowledge. And there *you* are. A nineteen-year-old first-year student with no advanced degrees, no letters after your name, no credentials. They're using words you've never even heard of before. What are the chances that you're right and these professors—nearly *all* of them—are wrong? I imagine you're beginning to think that the chances are pretty low.

These questions will begin to gnaw away at you, like a sliver in your mind, creating doubts about what you believe. So it's important to have an answer. It's critical to understand why the intellectual landscape is what it is. Here are some things to remember.

Just the Facts, Ma'am

We tend to think that we discover truth by simply gathering facts together. And once we've gathered enough facts, we can know things about the world. This includes knowledge about small things, such as who invented the cotton gin and how planes fly, as well as big things, such as the origins of the universe and the existence of God. It's all very "scientific," we think. To discover truth, you just have to put on the white lab coat and collect information.

Now, on this approach, truth becomes very "democratic." We tend to think that anyone can access truth (all one needs is facts) and that the people with the most facts are bound to be right.

But there happens to be a little problem here (and by little I mean big!). Science simply doesn't work this way. In 1962, the American philosopher Thomas Kuhn wrote a groundbreaking book titled *The Structure of Scientific Revolutions*. In that book he argued that science doesn't work in this linear "just the facts, ma'am" sort of way. Instead, facts are collected, sifted, and interpreted in light of a person's preexisting worldview—what Kuhn calls a "paradigm." And that worldview is not so much determined by the facts as it is controlling of what a person accepts as a fact in the first place.

While Kuhn's ideas have been tweaked and challenged over the years, the overall point of his work remains. And that point is remarkably simple: *people (including your professors) are not neutral.* They have a worldview, a paradigm, that shapes everything they see. Worldviews involve our most foundational commitments: where the world came from, our place in it, the purpose of life, the meaning of "right" and "wrong," the existence of God (or gods), what happens when we die, and so on. Although everyone has a worldview, most people have not really thought much about their own. It's just there in the background, conditioning and controlling their search for knowledge.

Having a worldview is kind of like wearing colored glasses.[1] Ever wore yellow sunglasses and then forgot you were wearing them? It affects everything you see, and you don't even realize it. What counts as green, red, and orange (not to mention yellow!) is distorted by the lenses through which you are looking. So a worldview is not so much something you look at as something you look *through*.[2]

Seeing What We Want to See

So what happens if a person's worldview is contrary to the way things actually are? Put differently, what if she is looking at the world through the *wrong* glasses? The answer is simple: she will misunderstand and misinterpret the data around her. And this will be the case no matter how smart she is and no matter how many Ivy League degrees she has.

Now this is not the time to make the case for why Christianity is the right worldview. That will happen as we go along (and is, in a sense, the point of all my letters to you). Right now I just want you to see that this explains why so many of your professors (and classmates) reject Christianity.

Think about it for a moment. If a person's worldview says miracles are impossible, he is unlikely to find the evidence for the resurrection convincing (no matter how good it might be!). If he believes that humans are born naturally good, then he is unlikely to think that all people everywhere (including him) need a Savior from their sins. And if he believes there is no God, then he is unlikely to affirm an objective moral code that we are all obligated to follow.

C. S. Lewis captured this reality well in his book *The Magician's Nephew*. While Narnia is a land filled with magic—where animals can talk and even sing—not all people can hear them. Indeed, Uncle Andrew cannot. When the animals speak to him, Uncle Andrew hears only animal sounds. Just noise, not words. Why? He is closed to the idea of a magical world. He assumes (in his worldview) that animals are nothing but dumb creatures.

Thus, when Aslan sings, Uncle Andrew is able to rationalize it away: "'Of course, it can't really have been singing,' he thought, 'I must have imagined it. I've been letting my nerves get out of order. Who ever heard of a lion singing?'"[3] Lewis (as the narrator) offers the most profound insight: "What you see and what you hear depends a great deal on where you are standing. It also depends on what sort of person you are."[4]

In other words, people accept only beliefs that are consistent with the *earlier and more foundational beliefs* present in their worldview.

To show how our prior beliefs affect the way we interpret the evidence, let me remind you of a crazy story from your childhood. When you were about eight years old, the whole family drove a couple of hours to my parents' house for Christmas Eve. That evening we planned to attend the Christmas Eve service at my home church—the church I grew up in. My parents departed for the service a little earlier than the rest of us (they were helping set up), and we planned to meet them there.

So later that evening we drove to church, parked the car, and Mom and I hustled you and your siblings into the church service. Also along were Uncle Scott and Aunt Jennifer with their four kids. We had a big crew and were worried about finding seats for all of us.

When we entered the lobby, I noticed that my church had installed a rather ornate water fountain (into which your cousins threw their Power Ranger figures!). The fountain seemed unusual, but I thought nothing of it. We entered the sanctuary and began looking for my parents, but for some reason we couldn't find them anywhere. I figured they must be busy talking to friends (though I couldn't find their friends either). After we finally found a seat, the service began with a formal processional down the center aisle. It included people in white robes and burning incense. As odd as that seemed to me, I figured that my home church must have grown more formal in the years since I left.

And then I saw it. Behind the pulpit, on the back wall of the sanctuary, hung a cross. But it wasn't just a cross; it was a *crucifix*—with a figure of Jesus hanging on it.

I looked at my brother, and he looked at me, and we both came to a rather shocking realization at the same moment. We were in the wrong church! Later we learned that in the years since we had moved away from home, a Roman Catholic church had been built right next door to our home church—even with similar architecture. And when we drove to the church that night, it was dark and foggy, explaining how we pulled into the wrong parking lot.

And here's the point I want you to see: There were tons of "facts" that should have shown me that I was in the wrong church—holy water in the lobby, parents nowhere to be found, no one I actually knew in sight, robes and incense, and even a crucifix on the wall. But I simply dismissed (and reinterpreted) each of these pieces of evidence in light of my prior belief that I was in the right church. That's how powerful paradigms can be—so powerful, in fact, that I didn't even realize I was not in the home church I grew up in.

Needless to say, I grabbed you and your siblings and hustled out of that church as soon as we realized what was happening. We hoped the Catholic church was not too upset that your cousins had thrown their Power Rangers into the holy water!

Simple point: people interpret the facts according to their worldview. And if their worldview is wrong, they reach wrong conclusions. Sometimes we see what we want to see.

Born This Way?

In all this, I know there is probably an even larger question looming in the back of your mind. Why do so many people walk around with a problematic worldview? What can explain why so many people have a paradigm that is hostile to Christianity?

Well, Christianity has an answer to that question. As strange as it might sound, the Bible teaches that people are *born* with a problematic worldview. That doesn't mean, of course, that people are born with a complete package of beliefs. Obviously, such beliefs are acquired over time, whether it's the Buddhist monk in China, the new age mystic in Romania, or the devout Muslim in the Middle East. At the same time, however, all people are born with an inherent disposition against the one true God. Because of Adam's sin, all humanity is born with a dark, fallen heart. And that fundamental reality very much shapes our belief systems.

This means that, apart from the Spirit's help, *people are hardwired to reject Christianity*. Paul makes this plain in his first letter to the Corinthians. He states, "The natural person does not accept the things of the Spirit of God, for they are folly to him, and he is not able to understand them" (1 Cor. 2:14). It's not just that non-Christians don't understand Christianity; they are *unable* to understand it. Christianity just seems foolish.

It's worth noting that the situation of the Corinthian church, to which Paul writes, is not that different from your own at UNC. Corinth had become quite the hub of intellectual thought. Not far from Athens, Corinth prided itself on the sophistication of its philosophers, analyzing the latest ideas that passed their way. It was a hotbed of ideas and debate—similar in many ways to the modern university.

In other words, the Christians in Corinth probably felt intellectually alone too, just like you do. No doubt, they also wondered why all the smartest people in their midst rejected Christianity. Maybe they even asked the same question you are asking: "Isn't it more likely that these brilliant philosophers are right and we Christians are wrong?"

But Paul is very clear: regardless of how smart people are, they cannot see the truth unless the Spirit opens their eyes. Thus, the widespread rejection of Christianity by intellectual elites *has nothing to do with whether Christianity is true.*

Once you realize that people need the Holy Spirit to understand Christianity, then a couple of implications follow. First, it helps you realize that disagreements with your non-Christian friends cannot be solved simply by giving them more facts. Regardless of how many good arguments you give them, they will always reinterpret the evidence in light of their worldview. What they ultimately need, therefore, is *conversion*—and only the Spirit can do that.

This doesn't mean that we don't present our best evidence and arguments for Christianity—we can and should. But it should temper our expectations. And, more importantly, it should lead us to pray for our non-Christian friends.

But there's a second implication. It also explains why *you* are a Christian. Paul is very keen to make sure the Corinthians understand something: they are not Christians because they are smarter than everyone else. On the contrary, Paul reminds the Corinthians, "Not many of you were wise according to worldly standards" (1 Cor. 1:26). In other words, they are believers because, and only because, God lavished his *grace* on them.

The same is true for you, Emma. You are a very smart girl, but that is not why you are a Christian. That's not why anyone is a Christian. You are a Christian solely because God graciously opened your eyes by the Holy Spirit so you could understand his word and his world. And that should lead to humility and thankfulness.

You're Not Really Alone

Sometimes the reason we feel intellectually alone is because we lack perspective. Fixated on the circumstances around us—living in a secular, post-Enlightenment world—we can forget that things were not always this way. Nor are they this way everywhere.

For example, it is helpful to remember that Christianity is, in fact, the world's largest religion, with adherents in the billions. Sure, not everyone bearing the label actually believes the core Christian doctrines, but many, many do. Thus, if you think globally, you are not alone. But even if you think just about the United States, nearly 41 percent regard themselves as evangelicals or "born again" Christians.[5] Atheism tracks at only 3 percent.[6]

What's the point? Outside Chapel Hill, things look very different.

Of course, the skeptic could always say that most of these people claiming to be Christians are uneducated and rural—especially in South America and Africa—and therefore don't really count. Aside from the condescending nature of such a view, however, you should be encouraged to know that many great intellectuals have embraced Christianity. This includes renowned scientists from history such as Johannes Kepler, Blaise Pascal, and Robert Boyle and also more modern scholars such as C. S. Lewis, Alvin Plantinga, and N. T. Wright. And we shouldn't forget the great thinkers of the early church like Ambrose, Augustine, and Jerome. They were the grand intellectuals of their day.

So, you may wonder, if there are great Christian thinkers out there, then why aren't more of them teaching at places like UNC? Well, this brings us back to the way worldviews work. If a university system is dominated by people with a non-Christian worldview, those people tend to hire others who share their worldview. Or at least they are unlikely to hire people who have a worldview they deem to be intellectually deficient and even offensive (which is what many think of the Christian worldview). As Greg Lukianoff and Jonathan Haidt observe in their book *The Coddling of the American Mind*, the lack of "viewpoint diversity" in modern universities creates a culture that is "vulnerable to group think and orthodoxy."[7]

Indeed, this bias against Christian scholars begins long before someone is interviewed for a job. It begins even in the admissions process to PhD programs. For example, when it comes to doctoral programs in religious or biblical studies, those with evangelical convictions face an uphill battle to get admitted, even if they have excellent academic credentials. Many evangelicals are sifted out of the process from the very start. As a result, many evangelical scholars don't end up at places like UNC but teach at evangelical institutions that are comfortable with their beliefs.

So beware of religion professors who defend their position by saying things such as "all scholars agree" or by saying that their view is "standard fare" among biblical scholars. What that really means is that their view is standard fare among all the scholars they already agree with (which, if you think about it, is not an overly significant point).

Overlooked in such claims are the thousands of evangelical scholars around the world who would disagree. You should know, for example, that the top ten largest seminaries in the United States are all evangelical. These seminaries represent thousands and thousands of students and hundreds and hundreds of professors. If virtually all scholars agree with your religion professor, then who are all these professors teaching at the ten largest seminaries? It is not so difficult for a professor to argue that their views are mainstream when they get to decide what is mainstream.

Remember, then, that you are not alone. Many people have believed what you believe, both in the past and in the present.

———

Emma, I hope you've been encouraged by the reminders above. Yes, it sometimes seems like we are the only ones who believe. And yes, that intellectual isolation can make us think that everyone else must be right, especially our professors. But truth is not determined by majority vote. One must view the world through a God-given lens to understand it rightly. And that can happen only by the help of the Holy Spirit.

I leave you with a reminder that you are not alone. Hear the words of Joshua: "Be strong and courageous. Do not be frightened, and do not be dismayed, for the LORD your God is with you wherever you go" (Josh. 1:9).

Love,

Dad

3

There Are a Lot of Different Views Here—How Can We Say That Christianity Is the Only Right Religion?

Right is right, even if nobody does it. Wrong is wrong even if everybody is wrong about it.

G. K. CHESTERTON

Dearest Emma,

One of the most exciting things about the college experience is the exposure to so many different kinds of people and their various systems of belief. If variety is the spice of life, there's plenty of it to be found at UNC. By now you are probably overwhelmed (and even exhilarated) by the scope and extent of the diversity that surrounds you. It's like being plunged into the Amazon rain forest and beholding a complex ecosystem filled with beautiful creatures you didn't even know existed.

There's the hard-core atheist-naturalist on your hall who thinks the universe is just matter in motion, with no God or transcendent being. There's the devoted Taoist in your economics class who is committed to Eastern meditation and self-discovery. There's the LGBT activist whose life purpose is to denounce any and all forms of "discrimination" on the basis of people's sexual identities. There's the suite mate who is into Oprah-style "spirituality" but not into any organized form of religion. And of course, there are countless students who have given very little thought to what they believe or why they believe it.

And then there's you. Like everyone else, you, too, have a set of beliefs about the world, God, morality, and so on. You are part of the ideological diversity at UNC. But there's one major difference. As a committed Christian, you believe there's only one true God and that all people are called to worship him and him alone. You don't believe that Christianity is just one of many good religious options. You don't believe, as Mahatma Gandhi once said, that "religions are different roads converging to the same point."[1]

In other words, your religious beliefs are *exclusive*.

But this will create problems. In a culture committed to relativism and tolerance, few things are more offensive than the claim that there's only one right religion. Years ago, I remember watching Oprah Winfrey interview Tom Cruise about his religion of Scientology. It was clear that she was skeptical about his religion, and Cruise was doing his best to explain it. And then she asked her most pointed question: "So Scientologists don't believe their way is the only way?"

You could feel the tension in the interview increase dramatically. Cruise's answer to that one question would determine everything. Surely he could never believe his religion is the only right one, could he? Who could ever believe *that*?

Cruise gave the culturally acceptable answer: "No. We're here to help. It's not like you've got to believe this, . . . [that] you must believe what I believe."[2] As soon as he said this, it seemed like the pressure in the interview evaporated. As long as you don't believe *that*, then all is well.

So what's problematic about believing one's religion is the only right one? Why is that such a big deal? Here are some of the objections you will hear.

Aren't Christians Just Arrogant Know-It-Alls?

To some, it seems incredibly *arrogant* for Christians to claim that their way is the only way. Who are *you* to say such a thing? Who do you think *you* are? Aren't Christians supposed to be humble? The strident atheist Christopher Hitchens captured this sentiment well when he declared that it was "fantastically arrogant" for someone to claim to know the mind of God.[3]

Now, some Christians feel the emotional weight of such questions. They don't want to be arrogant know-it-alls, so they feel obligated to soften the exclusive claims of Christianity. Maybe Christianity is not the only way after all, they might think. Maybe it's just one good option among many.

And, Emma, you will be tempted by this pathway. You have a gentle, soft spirit that does not like to offend others (and that's a good thing!). And you may feel like the better way forward is to try to make Christianity *less* exclusive. But you must remember that the claim that Christ is the only way is not arrogant. And here's why.

Lurking behind the charge that Christians are arrogant is a certain assumption about the way religion works. Many non-Christians view "religion" as merely *human attempts to discover and learn things about God*. Religion is simply the act of humans trying to figure out the divine. That means that whatever religious knowledge people have is due to their own religious efforts—their commitment, their zeal, their devotional acts. Moreover, that religious knowledge (because it is due to human effort) is inevitably flawed and fallible.

On this definition of religion, the Christian claim would indeed be arrogant! We would basically be claiming that we are the only ones who are smart enough and devoted enough to figure out what God is really like. Sadly, there are even many well-intended Christians today who have this incorrect view of religion, which is why so many of them feel sheepish about the Christian claim to exclusivity. But this is not the historical Christian understanding of the way our religion works. In fact, this human-driven view of religion is the *opposite* of the Christian claim.

As discussed in my prior letter, we do not claim to have true knowledge of God because we are better or smarter or more devoted than all other people. Our knowledge doesn't come from our efforts to figure out God but rather is the result of God graciously *revealing* himself to us. For Christianity, religion is not about humans finding God but about God showing himself to humans. It is about God seeking out lost sinners and opening their eyes to the truth. That is the opposite of an arrogant claim.

It is important to remember that a given claim is not arrogant simply because it is a "big" claim or is significant in its scope or impact. The arrogance or nonarrogance of a claim depends on whether one has adequate *grounds* for that claim. And Christians have solid grounds for believing Jesus is the only way, namely, because he *told us* in his word that he's the only way! Jesus said, "I am the way, and the truth, and the life. No one comes to the Father except through me" (John 14:6).

Is it arrogant simply to believe what Jesus has said about himself? Not at all. It is his claim, not our claim. We are merely passing it along.

The real objection, then, is about Jesus. Everything comes down to what people think about him, not what they think about us. Is *he* arrogant to claim that he is the only way to God? Well, that depends on the identity of Jesus. He didn't claim to be a mere human or simply a prophet but rather the divine Son of God. And as such, he would certainly have the authority to tell us about how one goes to heaven.

Aren't All Religions the Same?

But there is another (and perhaps weightier) objection to the Christian claim to exclusivity. Aside from whether Christians are arrogant, some folks object on the grounds that *all religions are basically the same*. Why should we think Christianity is the only right way when all religions offer the same moral message about loving others and being a good person? Sure, there are minor theological variations, but aren't all religions working toward the same goal, namely, to make the world a better place?

At first glance, such reasoning sounds quite plausible. Indeed, it makes Christians seem like quarrelsome folks who are needlessly picking a fight with all other religions. But a closer look reveals that this is not the case at all. First, all religions are decidedly *not* the same. They have major and irreconcilable differences. Some religions believe in only one God, others in multiple gods. Both can't be true. Some religions believe that the Qur'an is the word of God; others think it is not. Both can't be true. Some religions say hell exists; some say it doesn't. Both can't be true. Some say Jesus rose from the dead; others say he is still in the grave. Both can't be true.

The inescapable fact is that not all these religions can be right. Some of them have to be wrong.

I think most people at UNC, when pressed, would even admit this. Rhetorically, they push for the "all religions are the same" approach, but when faced with the harsh realities of some religions, they quickly change their tune. We know, for example, that many ancient religions practiced child sacrifice—from the worshipers of the Canaanite god Molech all the way to the religion of the Incas. Are we obligated to accept all these religions as equally valid as all others? Surely not. And I doubt many of your UNC friends are ready to affirm the truth of the various alien-inspired religions out there, such as Brazil's Sunrise Valley religion with its eight hundred thousand followers who believe they are aliens in human form! Thus, even postmodern folks eventually must admit that not every religious system can be correct.

Second, there are features about Christianity that make it genuinely distinct from the rest of the world's religions. And the fundamental difference is this: *Christianity is not just another religion about being a good person.* Needless to say, this flies in the face of what most people think about religion. Just consider the very popular television show *The Good Place*, starring Kristen Bell. As strange as it sounds, the show is a comedy about heaven (the good place) and hell (the bad place). On the show, the good place is where good people go, regardless of their religious beliefs. Whether you're Hindu, Buddhist, or Muslim, you go to the good place as long as your good deeds outweigh your bad.

In contrast, Christianity says something stunning. Something counterintuitive. Something unique. It says that *bad people go to the good place.* Just let that sink in for a moment. Heaven is not for good people but for sinful people forgiven by grace. Now, to be clear, God does care about how we live. In a sense, we could say that Christians are called to be "good people" by the help of the Spirit. But God's commandments are to be kept not as a mechanism of salvation (like so many other religions) but as an act of thanksgiving for the grace and mercy shown to us. We are not saved *by* obedience. We are saved *for* obedience.

The bottom line is this: we cannot be good enough to repair our broken relationship with God. Moralism is not the solution. It's the problem.

It is here that Christianity is genuinely different. The problem of our sin is solved not by us trying harder or becoming better but by God himself coming to earth in the flesh to live a righteous life and to die for the sins of his people. In other words, the solution is something that no other religion has (or could have): the person of Jesus Christ.

This reality highlights *why* Christianity is exclusive. Christianity does not claim to be the only way merely because we Christians are proud of ourselves or because we are looking for a way to promote our religion over all the others. No, Christianity claims to be the only way because it is the *only religion that offers a real solution to the problem of sin.* It is the only religion that offers an atoning sacrifice that pays the debt we owe.

Thus, there is an internal logic to why Christianity is exclusive. Think about it for a moment. If there were another way to heaven, then why did Jesus have to die? Why would he go through such a horrific death if heaven could be attained simply by following, say, the Eightfold Path of Buddhism? This is why Peter could confidently declare in Acts, "There is salvation in no one else, for there is no other name under heaven given among men by which we must be saved" (4:12).

Aren't All Truth Claims Relative?

Even if some of your UNC friends admit that not all religions are the same, they likely have another objection to Christianity's exclusive claims. They might argue that Christianity can't be the only true religion because all truth claims are relative anyway. You will hear statements like "Christianity might be *your* truth, but that doesn't mean it is *my* truth."

In other words, something can be true for one person and not true for another person. Truth is not objective but *personal*. Truth is not something "out there" to be discovered and observed; rather, truth comes from within, determined by each individual and each culture.

This whole approach—known as *relativism*—appears at first glance to be very levelheaded and reasonable. It sounds modest, even humble, to say things like "There's no religion that is more true than another." Indeed, it even seems like a convincing recipe for peace—no need to argue over religion if they are all equally "true"!

But relativism runs into some serious—in fact, insurmountable—intellectual problems. For example, you will notice that it is not (nor can be) followed consistently by its own advocates. Sure, relativism sounds good when you are dealing with religious issues, but what about other aspects of life? Can the statement "The earth is round" be true for one culture but not another? If a doctor says a person has cancer, will he respond by saying, "That's *your* truth, not *my* truth"? Common sense tells us that relativism simply doesn't work.

Of course, the skeptic could try to restrict his relativism to religious matters only. But there are problems with that too. Christianity makes objective *historical* claims that can be only either true or false. For example, when it comes to whether Jesus rose bodily from the grave, one cannot say, "That's true for you but not for me." Either Jesus rose or he didn't. And what individuals personally believe (or feel) will not change that fact.

But there's an even bigger problem for relativism—a fatal flaw, if you will. Relativism ends up being *self-contradictory*. The statement "There is no objective truth" is itself an objective truth claim. Put differently, relativism only works if the statement "There is no objective truth" is objectively true. Thus, relativism only works if it exempts itself from its own rules.

Relativism, therefore, is the equivalent of saying something like "All sentences are false." But if *all* sentences are false, then that very sentence is also false.

Incredibly, most relativists don't see the enormous inconsistency in their own position. Consider this statement by the popular Indian spiritualist Sri Chinmoy: "False religions will find fault with other religions; they will say that theirs is the only valid religion and their prophet is the only saviour. But a true religion will feel that all the prophets are saviours of mankind."[4] Essentially, Chinmoy is saying it is wrong to tell other religions that they are wrong. But isn't he doing the very thing he forbids? He's telling all those religions that claim to be right that they're wrong. Indeed, he even calls them "false religions"! It makes little sense to chide others for being intolerant and dogmatic if you turn around and do it yourself.

Here's the main point: in order for relativists to condemn others for making absolute truth claims, they must make their own absolute truth claims (namely, that there are no absolute truths). Thus, what seemed to be a humble position ends up being as dogmatic and absolutist as the positions it condemns.

Put bluntly, relativism is pride masquerading as humility. It operates like the gods Zeus and Hermes in Greek mythology—who would often disguise themselves as ordinary peasants in their dealings with mankind. What seemed to be a humble mortal on the outside was actually a divine figure on the inside.

Blind Leading the Blind

As an illustration of the way relativists disguise their own dogmatic claims, let me remind you of a family trip back in 2015. In the fall of that year, we took a short trip to the mountains of North Carolina and visited the Biltmore Estate, one of the largest historical homes in America. That year, they had an art exhibit that included a number of fascinating pieces.

But one piece stood out from the rest. It was a sculpture of an elephant with several blind men crawling around it, feeling its various body parts. You were confused (understandably!) about this strange exhibit, and you asked me what it was about. I told you that the sculpture was capturing a well-worn analogy about the way religion works.

Religion, relativists say, is like blind men feeling different parts of an elephant. As the blind men try to determine what an elephant is like, one feels the trunk and says, "An elephant is like a snake!" Another feels the tail and says, "An elephant is like a rope!" Another feels a leg and says, "An elephant is like a tree trunk!" And so, the argument goes, they are all right because they are each seeing only *part* of the truth. That's the way religion works.

But the core problem with the elephant analogy is that the person using the analogy is assuming that she sees the *whole* elephant. The person using the analogy is clearly not blind! She is basically saying, "Let me tell you how all religions *really* work." But that is an enormous claim that requires near-omniscient knowledge. How would this person know how all religions work? And why should this person be exempt from the very analogy she just gave?

Once again, what looks like a modest claim (namely, that religions are seeing only part of the truth) actually turns out to be quite a dogmatic one.

Of course, Christians claim to know the way religion really works. But here's the difference. We don't base that claim on our own efforts to figure out God. Rather, we believe that God has revealed himself to us by grace. Or, to put it differently, we think the elephant speaks. Unlike the analogy in which the elephant is silent—leaving it up to blind men to figure him out—Christians believe that God has plainly told us what he is like. And there is nothing arrogant about simply believing what God has said about himself.

Isn't Disagreement the Same as Disrespect?

Looming in the background of this whole discussion is the issue of how to treat those of different religious persuasions. Your fellow students at UNC—influenced, no doubt, by people like Sri Chinmoy—will say that we are not allowed to tell adherents of another religion that they are wrong because that would be an act of hostility and aggression. To say another religion is wrong is the first step toward violence and atrocity.

But again, this is a profound misunderstanding of the way Christians think. The claim that Jesus is the only way does not mean Christians are out to denigrate, demean, or despise adherents of other religions. On the contrary, we are called by Christ to show kindness, patience, and grace to all people—even (and perhaps especially) to those with whom we disagree. We can tell Hindus that they are mistaken and still treat them with dignity. Disagreement is not the same as disrespect.

Unfortunately, our postmodern world has come to equate these two things. For many people, disagreement *is* a form of disrespect—which goes a long way toward explaining the hostility toward Christianity. And this has profoundly affected the university environment. In prior generations, it was expected that intellectual engagement involved efforts to persuade others of the rightness of your view. Vigorous give-and-take was a normal part of the academic world. In fact, such interaction was actually a sign of respect, not disrespect; it meant you were taking another person's views seriously enough to engage them.

But not anymore. Under the banner of "tolerance," it is becoming harder and harder to disagree with someone. We are required to adopt a relativistic view of truth so that no one is ever offended by what we might say. Indeed, this has led to a profound crisis over free speech on the university campus. Rather than a healthy exchange of ideas, campuses are now more interested in safe spaces free of all microaggressions and triggers.[5]

This means that you need to be prepared to experience hostility from people as you try to share what you believe. In some cases, you might even be mocked and shamed for affirming that Christ is the only way. But stand your ground. And always do so with kindness. It's the *combination* of these two things that is so powerful. Some Christians stand their ground but are unkind to those who disagree. Other Christians are kind to those who disagree but abandon their belief that Christ is the only way. You are called to do *both*—stand your ground on the uniqueness of Christ and show kindness. The two are not mutually exclusive but belong together.

———

It is hard to stand for truth in a relativistic world. But remember *why* Christians believe Christ is the only way. It's not because we think we're smarter or better than other people but because we trust what

Jesus has revealed about himself. He's the very thing that makes Christianity unique. He's the only way that people can have their sins forgiven.

And don't believe all the rhetoric about how truth is relative. It sounds modest and humble to speak that way. But in the end, relativists are making their own dogmatic claims about the way religion works. And they are making such dogmatic claims without any foundation for their views beyond their own fallen, fallible minds.

If you want to find the truth, remember the words of Jesus: "If you abide in my word, you are truly my disciples, and you will know the truth, and the truth will set you free" (John 8:31–32).

Love,

Dad

My Christian Morals Are Viewed as Hateful and Intolerant—Shouldn't I Be More Loving and Accepting?

There is no good and evil, there is only power.
VOLDEMORT

Dearest Emma,

As I mentioned in my prior letter, diversity is the name of the game at UNC. There are a bewildering number of religious and philosophical views all around you. But by now, you've begun to realize that the diversity at UNC is not just intellectual. It's not only about what people believe but also about how they behave. Yes, there are many different worldviews out there, but there are also many different *systems of morality* that go along with those worldviews.

Of course, college campuses have never been known as bastions of moral virtue. The party atmosphere and near-hedonistic tendencies of modern university life are well known (as captured in all the 1980s movies I watched growing up). Even so, something has shifted—and shifted dramatically—in the last generation. And this shift is most evident in the way people approach the issue of sex and sexuality.

Now, part of that shift involves an increased willingness among college students to engage in sexual activity that prior generations may have been more hesitant about. Instead of just the occasional student willing to "sleep around," many modern universities now suffer from an entrenched hookup culture in which casual, unattached sexual encounters are so common that it makes prior generations look downright prudish.

In her book *The End of Sex: How Hookup Culture Is Leaving a Generation Unhappy, Sexually Unfulfilled, and Confused about Intimacy*, Donna Freitas documents this disturbing trend and its negative effects with alarming clarity.[1] And there is little doubt that this trend is driven, at least in part, by a broader culture steeped in pornography and more open to sexual experimentation (including homosexuality and transgenderism) than ever before.

But, believe it or not, this is only part of the sexual shift that has taken place in the last generation. The bigger—and more concerning—part is the shift in people's *attitude* toward their sexual activity. No longer is sex just something people *do*, it is viewed as core to who they *are*. People have attached their "identity" to their sexual activity and their sexual preferences. The two—sex and identity—are now inextricably intertwined.

This bigger shift has tremendous implications for you on the college campus. It means that your views on morality—especially as they pertain to sex—will be seen as a personal attack on people. While in prior generations the biblical view of sex would have just been viewed as old-fashioned and stodgy, now it is viewed as downright hateful and discriminatory. It's regarded not as just a different opinion but as a full-frontal assault on another person's dignity and worth.

In other words, much of the world considers your view of sex—more to the point, the Bible's view of sex—as *immoral*. (Just let the irony of that sink in for a moment).

And here's what's going to happen (and probably already has happened). You will begin to doubt the goodness and rightness of your moral positions. You may wonder if *you* are the problem. You may begin to feel like you're a hateful, discriminatory person. And this might tempt you to change your views so that you are seen as more "loving" and "tolerant."

Don't underestimate the danger here. Many a well-intended Christian has gone off to college with a biblical view of sex and been crushed by the relentless disapproval of the university culture. Over time, that takes a toll. And this is why so many Christian college students, sadly, have changed their views on sex. It is hard to hold on to a view when you are persistently told it is hateful and unloving.

But, of course, that is the key question. Is biblical morality *really* hateful and unloving? And how does one determine what is moral or immoral in the first place? Those are the issues that I want to address in this letter.

Everyone Is a Fundamentalist

The primary complaint about Christian morality is that it is absolute. Christians have the audacity to think that the moral commands of the Bible apply not only to them but to all humans. And it is this very thing, at least in today's culture, that makes Christians so judgmental. They try to *impose* their moral code on others.

And why is this a problem? Well, your fellow students at UNC will argue that it's a problem because morality doesn't work that way. Morality is not absolute but subjective; what is right for one person is not necessarily right for another. In other words, morality is *relative* (there's that word again), varying from person to person and culture to culture. Which is precisely why Christians need to keep their moral objections to themselves.

Once again, this line of reasoning has a surface-level plausibility to it. Maybe morality is like music or art—what works for one person just doesn't work for another. But upon closer scrutiny, moral relativism runs into a number of serious (and, I would argue, fatal) problems.

First, there's the question of how your fellow students *know* that morality is relative. They say it confidently and repeatedly, but what are the *grounds* for their claim? If you think about it, moral relativists are making an enormous claim. Essentially, they are declaring that they have figured out one of the deepest mysteries of the universe—indeed, one of the most perplexing aspects of our existence—which is the meaning of right and wrong and of good and evil. And your nineteen-year-old friends have stood up to basically declare, "Well, we've got this one figured out. Right and wrong are just subjective entities; there's no objective good and evil. Nothing to see here. Move along."

But, of course, you know it's not that simple. In order to make such a grand, sweeping claim about the universe, one would have to know a lot about it. How does your classmate know that there can be no moral absolutes in the universe? Has she searched it out extensively? Has she examined every aspect of it? Does she have omniscient knowledge?

Obviously, no college student (no human) has done any of these things. Moral relativism is just something people say is true, but you will discover they have no reason for knowing it's true. They declare it confidently, expecting everyone just to agree. But in the end, it is an arbitrary claim. It's more about what they *wish* were true.

The next time someone says morals are relative, just ask, "So tell me, how do you *know* morals are relative?" You might be surprised by the blank stares you receive.

Second, moral relativists are profoundly *inconsistent*. They talk about how morals are subjective, but their actions go the opposite direction. Indeed, the very people who insist on moral relativism are often the same ones delivering the most scathing moral con-demnations of other people's behavior. The very people who insist that Christians should keep their morals to themselves are often the ones proclaiming their own moral objections the most loudly.

If you listen carefully to your fellow students, you will see this pattern. In one moment, they talk about how morality varies from person to person, and in another, they condemn the treatment of migrant families at the border as "wrong." Which one is it? In one moment, they talk about how Christians shouldn't impose their moral code on others, but then in the next, they are insisting that everyone should accept and approve of homosexual marriage. Isn't that imposing a moral belief? In one moment, they insist that each culture gets to determine its own ethical norms, but then in the next, they are condemning foreign cultures for their views of women. How can they do both?

Here's the point: moral relativists often act in direct opposition to their own stated position. Now, you may wonder why they do that. Why flip-flop? The answer is found in the next problem.

Third, if moral relativism were really the case, then it would un-dercut our ability to object to *any* moral atrocity. We might not like what Hitler did to the Jews, but we couldn't say it was *really* wrong because, after all, right and wrong are subjectively determined by each culture. We may not prefer the behavior of Dylann Roof when he massacred nine African Americans inside their church, but we couldn't say it is *really* wrong. If everyone can create their own system of right and wrong, then Dylann Roof can do it too.

Essentially, then, moral relativists would be forced to agree with Voldemort: "There is no good or evil, there is only power." *This* is why moral relativists flip-flop. Their moral relativism leads to an irrational existence. And they're looking for a way out.

Ironically, this current generation (your generation, Emma) has begun to realize this problem more and more. Even though they say morals are relative, they are actually driven by a deep *moral outrage* over the wrongs they see in the world—polluting the environment, sexual abuse, systemic racism. And this moral outrage has created what David Brooks of the *New York Times* has called a "shame culture."[2] Any dissenters or violators of the new moral order are quickly castigated online and shunned through social media. In many ways, this is a strange new form of religious fundamentalism. As Samuel James observes, "The modern campus culture is a religious culture, but it's a religion without God."[3]

Now does this mean that the age of moral relativism is over and that a new age of moral absolutism has replaced it? I don't think so. The fact of the matter is that most of your friends are both moral relativists and moral absolutists *at the same time*. For some behaviors, they are one; for other behaviors, they are the other. They pick and choose. So when it comes to environmentalism and the treatment of refugees, they abandon moral relativism and act as if there are moral absolutes after all. But when it comes to their sexual behavior, then they suddenly become moral relativists again, insistent that morality is determined by each person and culture. They want to have it both ways.

But in the end, moral relativists find themselves on the horns of a dilemma. Either they go "all in" on their moral relativism and really follow it consistently, or they just admit that there are moral absolutes after all. When pressed, I think most of your UNC friends will go with the latter option. They know that some things are just objectively wrong, regardless of what other people say or feel about it.

But this does raise an additional question: *If there really are moral absolutes in the universe, where do they come from?* Here's where things get really interesting.

Can You Have Morality apart from God?

So if there are moral absolutes in the world after all—so that certain behaviors are right or wrong, regardless of what people feel and think about them—what can account for their existence? And if they do exist, how can we know what they are?

It might surprise you, but most people who make dogmatic moral claims never even consider such questions. They just make a claim like "What Harvey Weinstein did to all those women was *evil*" without asking what makes a certain act "evil" in the first place. But if you think about it, calling a behavior "evil" implies that there's some *standard* out there that the perpetrator failed to live up to. It implies that there's some rule that has been violated. But where does this standard or rule come from?

Well, if you reflect on that question for a moment, you will quickly realize that several things have to be true of the standard for moral absolutes. First, the standard has to be absolute itself. It has to be the *ultimate* standard for goodness. Why? Imagine if we tried to use a standard that was not ultimate goodness—a standard that was a *mix* of good and evil. For one, that would be not a reliable guide to morality but a limited and flawed one. Moreover, we would only know that this standard was a mix of good and evil if there were still some *higher* standard by which we judged it. And if there's an even higher standard above it, then *that* should be our ultimate moral guide.

Second, our standard for moral absolutes has to be independent of, and bigger than, human opinion. If our standard for moral absolutes were merely what one person or one culture happened to think about morals, then obviously those morals could not be absolute. The only way to prevent morality from being subjective (and ever changing) is to have a standard that supersedes human experience and stands over it. Put bluntly, the standard for human morality cannot be something (or someone) that is merely human.

Third, our standard for moral absolutes must be personal. Think about it for a moment. Can moral norms come from a universe that is utterly impersonal, composed only of matter? Not at all. Material objects—rocks, trees, minerals, atoms—cannot impose moral obligations on humans. They cannot determine whether one act is "right" and another "wrong." They cannot demand loyalty or obedience. In a world that is only physical, what one bag of molecules does to another bag of molecules is utterly meaningless.

But what if our standard for morality was not impersonal but personal? The existence of moral obligations makes the most sense when a *relationship* is involved. The existence of another person—especially if that person is your Lord and Creator—*would* obligate us to behave one way or another.

Here's the big point: the source for moral absolutes has to be an absolutely good, transcendent, personal being. In other words, we would argue that *the only coherent foundation for moral absolutes is God himself.*

Needless to say, atheists have not gone quietly into the night over this issue. Some atheists have even taken personal offense, pointing out that many atheists do, in fact, live moral lives. Thus, atheist Richard Dawkins rejects "the preposterous idea that we need God to be good."[4] But such a response misses the point entirely. Christians have never argued that atheists cannot *be* good. On the contrary, the Bible teaches that people (even atheists) often act good because they have a built-in sense of morality owing to the fact that they are made in the image of God (Rom. 2:15). The problem for the atheist is not *being* moral but having adequate *grounds* for morality. In an atheistic world, there are not "good" acts and "bad" acts; there are just acts.

Another atheist response is to use evolution to explain the origins of morality. Humans have evolved into moral creatures, it is argued, because morality creates a better chance for cooperation, survival, and the promulgation of the species. But this explanation also misses the mark. For one, there are many behaviors that could help promulgate the species that many would still regard as morally problematic. For example, some studies have argued that rape is biologically advantageous for animals because it allows them to pass along their genetic material even if they cannot find a willing mate. But surely we would never conclude that rape is therefore a "good" thing! This highlights the main problem with evolutionary explanations for morals: such explanations might explain *why* humans engage in certain behaviors, but they never explain what makes that behavior really "good" or "bad" in the first place.

But evolutionary explanations for moral absolutes face an even bigger problem. If morals are the product of evolution, then that means they can change over time. Theoretically, then, different groups of humans could evolve with different (and contradictory) morals. We would have to admit that something like child sacrifice could be "good" within one group and "bad" within another. But that would make morality subjective and arbitrary, not absolute.

When all the dust settles in these sorts of discussions, we are left with an inescapable conclusion: only God can provide the necessary foundation for morality.

Rethinking Conversations about Morality

So far we've seen two things. First, everyone has moral absolutes (even if they say they don't) because we need them for a rational existence. And second, moral absolutes are grounded in the existence of God. So how should that affect your conversations about morality with your non-Christian friends?

For one, it reminds you that your moral views (particularly about sex) are not really your views at all; they are God's. That means that if people think your views are hateful, then they would have to think that God himself is hateful. If people get upset with you, just remember that they are really upset with the God you serve.

The goal of your conversations, therefore, will be not so much about helping your friends understand your views as about helping them understand *your God*. Help them see that God is absolutely good and that he gives us moral laws—even laws about sex—*for our good*. He doesn't provide laws to be mean or cruel or oppressive. But he gives them out of love, knowing that obedience is the path of life and disobedience the path of death.

When you were just a little toddler (that was a long time ago!), I can still remember that one of my biggest fears was that you would run out into a busy road. Sometimes little kids just take off running without looking where they are going. So I worked hard to train you to listen to my voice when I yelled "Stop!" Now, in the ears of a toddler, "Stop!" sounds like a mean parent keeping you from all the fun you are about to have. But in reality, "Stop!" was an act of love designed to keep you from getting hurt.

That's the way it is with God. He wants us to listen to his voice. It's not for our detriment but for our benefit. The reason we don't believe this is because we've been trained in our culture to think sin isn't that big of a deal. It won't really hurt us, we think. We'll be fine. But God knows better. Sin will only kill, steal, and destroy. Thus, it is an act of love to help your friends understand that their behavior is taking them down a harmful path.

Of course, this doesn't mean that you are always obligated to call out every sin you see at UNC. If you did that, you would have time for little else (and it would make you an unpleasant person to be around). But there will be times that you will need to stand up for what you know is right. And just remember, doing so does not make you hateful or cruel.

And here's one more tip for your conversations with your fellow UNC students. When discussing morality, don't get sidetracked by arguing over only *individual behaviors* and whether they are right or wrong. There may be a time to debate things like homosexual marriage or same-sex unions, but keep the focus of the conversation on the bigger and more foundational questions: How do you know whether *any* behavior is right or wrong? Where do morals come from in the first place?

If you do this, you will notice that your conversations will take a dramatic turn (in your favor). It will force your non-Christian friends to account for their *own* moral claims (which they are rarely asked to do). How can they make moral accusations against Christians (charging you with being "hateful") when they have no grounds for knowing what's moral or immoral in the first place?

In contrast, you can show them that Christians have a good standard for their moral views, namely, the character of the Creator as it is revealed in Scripture. Hopefully, this will cause them to reflect more deeply on why (and what) they believe.

———

It is hard to hear—over and over again—that your views on morality are hateful and intolerant. But you have to keep reminding yourself of what is true. God, not man, determines morality. He is a loving God, so we can trust that he knows best. And his word tells us, "His commandments are not burdensome" (1 John 5:3).

Your job is to believe that and to follow him.

Love,

Dad

5

I Have Gay Friends Who Are Kind, Wonderful, and Happy— Are We Sure That Homosexuality Is Really Wrong?

We all do no end of feeling, and we mistake it for thinking.
MARK TWAIN

Dearest Emma,

As I mentioned in my prior letter, your generation has experienced an enormous shift in the way it approaches sex and sexuality. People's sexual behavior and personal identity are linked together like never before. Thus, to reject a person's sexuality feels like a rejection of them. The two cannot be separated.

This problem will become particularly complicated as you get to know people who are gay and they become your friends. They might be frustrated (even angry) because they feel like you don't *really* love and accept them unless you approve of their behavior. Then you will begin to doubt what you believe, asking whether you might be mistaken about your view of sex. You might begin to wonder whether Christians could be wrong—or whether the Bible could be wrong—about a subject that seems so personal to you and your friends.

As you struggle through these issues, you're going to hear a lot of arguments for why you should accept homosexuality. And let me warn you, some of these arguments can be *emotionally* powerful. A person with a soft, kind heart like you (which, again, is a good thing) needs to sift through the arguments carefully, always trusting biblical reasoning and not your feelings.

So here are six arguments you will hear for why you should accept homosexuality. Let's work through them together, one at a time.

Homosexuals Are Kind, Caring, Wonderful People

One of the most common (and most powerful) reasons why people accept homosexuality is that they discover that many homosexuals are kind, wonderful people. Sometimes people change their view on homosexuality simply because they have homosexual friends whom they really *like*. Of course, your gay friends can be warm, thoughtful, funny, caring, and giving. Even more—and here's where things get really complex—it might seem that some of your homosexual friends are even kinder than some of your Christian friends.

Believe it or not, this has led many people to change their view on homosexuality. If it's such a bad thing, they reason, then how could such wonderful people be doing it? Or, put differently, if wonderful people engage in a behavior I think is wrong, then maybe I ought to rethink whether it is wrong.

But if we put our emotions on hold and really think about this argument, it falls apart pretty quickly. Effectively, the entire argument is built on the premise that something is wrong only if the people doing it are mean spirited and unpleasant. In other words, it assumes that the morality of an act is somehow connected to the character (or likability) of those who perform it.

This, however, is not the way Christians think about morality. Christians don't claim that something is wrong only if "really awful" people do it. We argue that something is wrong if it conflicts with God's character, which is reflected in his commandments. Thus, Christians would argue that it is very possible (and very common) for very nice people with many other wonderful virtues to be engaged in behavior that is very wrong.

In fact, there is a biblical explanation for why this is the case. All human beings are made in the image of God and have his law written on their conscience. Thus, all humans (including homosexuals) have the potential to perform great acts of kindness and virtue. But at the same time, all humans have a fallen, sinful nature and are capable of awful sins. In other words, human beings are a "mix" of virtue and vice.

Here's the other thing. If Christians change their view of homosexuality simply because they discover that homosexuals are nice people, then that actually reveals a very embarrassing reality, namely, that they had assumed homosexuals must be awful people. In other words, it reveals that they had a form of *prejudice*—they had assumed that people who are different from them must be mean, cruel, and unpleasant. But that is a decidedly anti-Christian way of thinking.

The true Christian position has never argued that homosexuality is wrong because homosexuals are such unpleasant people; rather, the Christian position is that even wonderful people can sometimes fall into serious sin. In other words, our objection to homosexuality is based not just on our *experience* with homosexuals but on the *principles* revealed in God's word. It's based not on emotion but on truth.

That means, Emma, that it's okay to have homosexual friends whom you think are kind, wonderful people and, at the same time, to believe homosexuality itself is sinful. The two are not mutually exclusive.

Homosexuals Are Just Looking for Love and Companionship

Another common argument in favor of homosexuality is to argue that homosexuals are merely seeking out love and companionship like the rest of us. And therefore to deny them such companionship is not only unfair but an act of cruelty. Christians are effectively condemning them to a life of singleness and loneliness. Why should homosexuals not be allowed to be with the ones they love? Everyone else gets to do that!

You can see why this sort of reasoning is so persuasive. It makes it seem that homosexuals are just seeking "love" (who could object to that?), and it paints Christians as the Ebenezer Scrooges of religion—we are just miserly people who hold back good things from everyone else. It's an emotional appeal that really works.

But it doesn't work as an actual argument. In essence, homosexuals are arguing that people should be able to be with *whomever they love*. But are they willing to follow that logic to where it leads? Can everyone be with the one they love? What if a father fell in love with his daughter; could they be together? What if a brother and sister fell in love; could they be together? What if a man fell in love with *three* women; could they all be together? What if a married woman fell in love with her coworker; should she leave her husband so they could be together? Common decency (not to mention the Bible) indicates that the answer to each of these questions is no.

Here's the point: the logic used to justify homosexual behavior—namely, that people should be allowed to be with whomever they love—could be used to justify virtually *any* sexual behavior.

The people using this argument, then, are on the horns of a dilemma. On the one side, they could admit that there have to be *some* boundaries. Sometimes doing the right thing means a person just can't be with the one he or she claims to love—even if it leaves a person single and alone. But then that undercuts their argument for why homosexual activity should be accepted. On the other side, they could advocate for no sexual restrictions whatsoever. But then they would be forced to accept incest, infidelity, polyamory, and more.

In the end, the "everyone should get to be with the one they love" argument just doesn't work. It proves either too much or too little.

Homosexuality Is Genetically Determined

Back in 2013, the rapper Macklemore released a very popular (and controversial) song in favor of gay marriage titled "Same Love." The lyrics of that song used a very common argument in favor of same-sex unions, namely, that people are *born* gay and can't change what they feel. The song says, "And I can't change / Even if I tried." Essentially, Macklemore is arguing that homosexuality is all right because people are hardwired this way—it's what he calls a "predisposition." There's no resisting who you really are. You can't change it. You just have to go with it.

This sort of argument picks up on a broader cultural theme that seems to be everywhere these days. And that theme is, essentially, *Be yourself.* Embrace who you are and stop trying to change who you are. Just think of the wildly popular song, "Let It Go," from the movie *Frozen.* Elsa is a person who is weary of putting up a front and finally embraces her true identity. It's a song about emancipation: "No right, no wrong, no rules for me, / I'm free."

So does this argument work? Are people really "born this way"? We can begin by acknowledging that there is an *element* of truth here. While there is no hard scientific evidence for a "gay gene," many homosexuals testify that they have been same-sex attracted for as long as they can remember, even back to their childhood days. Moreover, same-sex attraction is not something that can be easily turned off, like a light switch. Even for celibate homosexuals, a predisposition toward those of the same sex may persist for the rest of their life.

At the same time, however, we cannot use genetic predisposition as a basis for declaring a behavior to be "good" or "right." *Behaviors are not right simply because we are inclined to engage in them.* Alcoholics might be born with a predisposition to drink (and there is even better scientific evidence for this than for same-sex attraction), but I have never heard an Alcoholics Anonymous (AA) meeting proclaim alcoholism to be "right" as a result. Similarly, pedophiles will often declare that they were born with a sexual disposition toward children, but even if that were true, few would want to claim that therefore pedophilia is moral, right, and good. Sometimes it's right to resist a behavior, even if you are inherently drawn to it.

It should also be said that an inclination toward a behavior is not a basis for declaring that change is impossible. Remember Macklemore's words: "I can't change / Even if I tried." But what if an alcoholic said this? Wonder what his AA sponsor would say? Or can you imagine a serial adulterer saying these words: "I can't change, even if I tried." Wonder what his wife would say?

Even more, imagine giving that message to the youth of the day: "Please choose the right moral behavior. But if you discover that something is really attractive to you, and if you discover that it is difficult to avoid, then it must be okay. The only behaviors that are really immoral are the ones that you feel little inclination to follow."

Of course, that is nonsensical, and I think most people know it deep down. So here's the point: just because a certain behavior is difficult for someone to avoid is hardly grounds for declaring that someone should abandon his efforts—and it is certainly no basis for declaring it to be good!

Unfortunately, the reason our culture buys into this argument is that it has no concept of original sin. Our culture believes all people to be inherently good at their core. Thus, in most people's minds, it is always appropriate to tell someone, "Be yourself." After all, they believe their true self is good. But the Bible has a very different message. Our true self, apart from Christ, is *not* good. Indeed, we are corrupted by the original sin of Adam and are often inclined toward evil. You could even say we are "born this way." In such a scenario, you would want to be very careful about telling someone, "Be yourself." Indeed, given the corruption of sin, you might want to tell them, "*Don't* be yourself!"

This helps us understand the message of the gospel. The message of the gospel is not "Be yourself." You're not the solution; you're the problem. Instead, the message of the gospel is "Deny yourself"— turn away from your sins and follow Christ (cf. Matt 16:24). Or, from the bigger picture, we could say to someone, "You need a *new* self." This is essentially what Jesus told Nicodemus, "Unless one is *born again* he cannot see the kingdom of God" (John 3:3).

Homosexuality Is Not *Really* Condemned by the Bible

In years gone by, if a person embraced homosexuality, he realized that he would have to reject Christianity. The two simply didn't fit together, and most people understood that. But in recent years, things have shifted. A new "gay Christian" movement has arisen—driven by the writings of those like Matthew Vines—in which people have attempted to embrace both Christianity and homosexuality at the same time. The Bible is not *really* against homosexuality, we are told. It has just been misunderstood for thousands of years (until now, of course).

Just a limited familiarity with the Bible is enough to know that this argument lacks plausibility even on the surface. The Bible is very clear about sex and marriage, and it repeatedly and plainly teaches that homosexuality is outside God's design for sex.[1] While we lack space to review all that it says, here are a few reminders:

- The Bible speaks extensively about marriage, which is always limited to a man and a woman. This is not only clear from the very beginning of the Bible (Gen. 2:24–25) but also plainly affirmed by Jesus himself (Matt. 19:4–6). Yes, there are descriptions of biblical characters who have multiple wives, but mere descriptions are not endorsement. Such behavior is expressly condemned (Deut. 17:17; 1 Kings 11:2).
- Homosexual acts are routinely condemned both in Old Testament times (Lev. 18:22; 20:13) and also in New Testament times (Rom. 1:26–27; 1 Cor. 6:9–11; 1 Tim. 1:8–10). So one cannot argue that it is just an Old Testament issue. And the reason it is condemned is not hard to find: homosexuality is contrary to God's design and contrary to "nature" (Rom. 1:26).
- Homosexual practice is judged by God both at Sodom and Gomorrah (Gen. 19) and at Gibeah (Judg. 19). In the New Testament, Jude 7 reiterates that judgment fell on the people of Sodom and Gomorrah precisely for this reason: "[They]

indulged in sexual immorality and pursued *unnatural desire"*—a clear reference to homosexual activity.

Beyond these biblical passages, we should also remember that the Christian church, for two thousand years, has been united in its interpretation of them. In other words, the church throughout the ages has been consistent and unchanging in its teaching that homosexuality is outside God's design for sex. Don Fortson and Rollin Grams refer to this as an "amazing unanimity over centuries" concerning the church's unified approach to homosexuality.[2] It is only in the modern day—with the rise of the sexual revolution—that these biblical passages have been reinterpreted to match current cultural trends.

Homosexuality (Even If It's a Sin) Is Not a Big Deal

Even if a person concedes that homosexuality is a sin, you need to be ready for a follow-up argument. Some will say that Christians are making too big of a deal of the whole issue because homosexuality is no worse than other sins. After all, every sin is equal in God's sight, right? So Christians should stop talking about homosexuality until they are also willing to talk about gluttony or gossip or divorce or any other "acceptable" sin out there. If everyone is a sinner, then we are not allowed to highlight any particular sin.

Now, there is an element of truth in the idea that "every sin is equal." It is true that *any* sin is enough to separate us from God and warrant his judgment. No matter how trivial that sin might seem in our eyes—even eating forbidden fruit (Gen. 3:6)—it is a serious offense against a holy God.

But does that mean all sins are *equally bad*? Not at all. The Bible differentiates between sins in terms of their seriousness. Some sins are more severe in terms of impact (1 Cor. 6:18), in terms of culpability (Rom. 1:21–32), and in terms of the temporal judgment warranted (Mark 9:42; James 3:1; 2 Pet. 2:17).

Indeed, we intuitively make similar distinctions in our earthly legal systems. If a person gets in her car and runs over her neighbor's mailbox, she will get a very different penalty than if she runs over her neighbor. Both are crimes, but one is more severe than the other.

In terms of homosexuality, we would simply want to observe that the Bible describes it as one of the most serious sexual offenses. When Paul is looking for a key example of how God has "turned over" men to the lusts of their hearts, the example he picks is that of homosexuality: "God gave them up to dishonorable passions, . . . men committing shameless acts with men and receiving in themselves the due penalty for their error" (Rom. 1:26–27). And Leviticus puts homosexuality among the gravest of sexual sins, even referring to it as an "abomination" (Lev. 20:13). Moreover, homosexuality overturns God's design for marriage, a foundational institution that is core to human flourishing (Gen. 2:24–25) and designed to reflect the relationship between Christ and the church (Eph. 5:31–32).

Now, this does not mean that there's no hope for those who are caught in homosexuality. While Paul says that those who practice homosexuality will not enter the kingdom of God, he offers an encouraging observation, "And such *were* some of you. But you were washed, you were sanctified, you were justified in the name of the Lord Jesus Christ" (1 Cor. 6:11). This is what makes the gospel *good news*. No matter how big the sin, there is always forgiveness for everyone who repents and trusts in Jesus Christ for salvation.

Homosexuals Have Been Mistreated by Christians

Westboro Baptist Church. That is a name that conjures up images of picketing at funerals, antigay slurs, and profoundly cruel and uncaring treatment of homosexuals. And while few Christian groups are as extreme as Westboro Baptist, there are certainly others that have mistreated homosexuals in either attitude, tone, or practice.

So how should we respond to such harshness? First, we should be deeply saddened. Christians are called to treat all human beings with dignity and respect by virtue of the fact that they are made in the image of God. Even if there are deep disagreements over moral issues, we are still called to be kind and loving. And sadly, that has not always been the case.

That said, we would also want to correct the misconception that this behavior is typical of Christians or Christianity. It would be unfair to characterize the entire Christian movement by the isolated practices of some. Moreover, it is important to remember that Christians are often (wrongly) labeled as "cruel" or "hateful" simply because they affirm the historical Christian position on sexuality. Simply holding to the biblical view of sex does not make one guilty of oppressing and mistreating homosexuals.

And it is here that we cannot lose sight of the overall issue. Even if some Christians have not loved homosexuals as they ought, is that a valid argument for why we should accept homosexuality itself as morally good? Not at all. Whether homosexuals have been treated well or treated poorly has no bearing whatsoever on the moral status of homosexuality.

By way of illustration, imagine a group of corrupt police officers who handle cases of illegal drug users. After arresting the perpetrators, they typically "rough up" the addicts while they are in jail.

All would agree that such police officers are guilty of mistreating the prisoners. Indeed, such mistreatment is an egregious violation of their duty as officers. But do we address the mistreatment of prisoners by convincing all police officers that illegal drug use is not a crime after all? Of course not. Heroin, cocaine, and other such drugs can destroy the lives of both the user and the dealer. The mistreatment of addicts doesn't mean we suddenly want the addicts to continue their self-destructive behavior. We need to separate the morality of an act from the way we treat those who commit such an act.

But even though this argument doesn't work, it continues to be used. Why? Because it is *emotionally powerful*. And you need to understand this. Many Christians (rightly) feel bad about the way some homosexuals have been treated but then (wrongly) conclude that the best solution is to fully accept the goodness of homosexuality. Don't make this mistake. We can work hard to treat all people with dignity and respect, without compromising what God has revealed about sex in the Scriptures.

———

Emma, it's complicated having friends who are gay. You will feel the pressure to pick between your friendships or your moral convictions. And if it's one or the other, most people will end up picking their friends. But it's *not* one or the other. The Bible makes it clear that we can *really* love people—we can be kind, generous, and respectful—and also believe that they are caught in serious sin.

The perfect model of this approach is Jesus himself. When he met the rich young ruler, the passage tells us, "Jesus, looking at him, *loved* him" (Mark 10:21). And then, in the very next breath, Jesus confronted the man's idolatry of money: "You lack one thing: go, sell all that you have and give to the poor, and you will have treasure in heaven" (Mark 10:21).

Love *and* truth. It's not one or the other. It's both.

Love,

Dad

6

The Concept of Hell Seems Barbaric and Cruel—Wouldn't a Loving God Save Everyone?

There is one very serious defect to my mind in Christ's moral character, and that is that He believed in hell.
BERTRAND RUSSELL

Dearest Emma,

One of the things I love most about you is that you have a deep desire to share Jesus with those around you. God has given you a wonderful heart for the lost. In fact, we have seen this in you from a very young age. When you were in kindergarten, your Christian school had its annual Missions Week, focusing on God's love for the nations. You came back from that week so excited and said you wanted to be a missionary even at five years old!

And now, many years later, God has actually placed you on a mission field of sorts—the university campus. I know you will get plenty of opportunities to share your faith at UNC. And when you do, you will hear all sorts of objections to the gospel message.

I've already covered some of these in prior letters, but I want to mention another one. And this one is big.

You will share the gospel with some people who will object to the fundamental premise of Christianity, namely, that *everyone needs a savior*. They will bristle against the idea that they are under God's "wrath." They will insist that they are pretty good people. And therefore, the idea that people might suffer eternal judgment in hell is absolutely barbaric and unthinkably absurd. What sort of God would do such a thing? "*My* God would not do that," they will protest. "Isn't God supposed to be a God of *love*?"

Now, these sorts of objections may begin to take a toll on you personally. It's hard to deliver a message as good news when so many people take it as bad news. You may even begin to doubt what you think about concepts like judgment, sin, and hell. After all, you might wonder, why doesn't God just save everyone? Wouldn't that be better?

Sadly, some well-known authors in the Christian world have even begun to raise doubts about the doctrine of hell. In 2011, then-pastor Rob Bell published the book *Love Wins*, which argues that the idea of hell is "misguided and toxic."[1] His rhetoric sounds very much like what you will hear on the UNC campus: "Has God created billions of people over thousands of years only to select a few to go to heaven and everyone else to suffer forever in hell? Is this acceptable to God? How is this 'good news'?"[2] Determined to do away with this unpleasant doctrine, Bell then proceeds to argue for what is essentially a form of universalism. There is no literal hell, because, in the end, everyone will find their way back to God.

So we need to dive into these questions more deeply. And when we do, we will discover that the doctrine of hell, though challenging and difficult at times, actually makes sense when it is properly viewed within the context of the larger Christian worldview.

Hey, God, Good to Meet You

Here's the first thing you need to understand: most people have a very different view of God from the one presented in the Bible. Most people view God (if he exists at all) as a pretty affable fellow, generally laid back, who stays out of your business unless you need a little help. He's a bit like the cool, uninvolved parent who is not too worried about how you live your life "as long as you are happy."

Of course, in this view of God, the doctrine of hell is utterly absurd. Why would a God like *this* ever judge anyone? Once again, you can see why worldviews play such a big role in these sorts of debates. Whether a person believes in hell is contingent on the *earlier and more foundational beliefs* in their worldview about who God is, what he's like, and so on.

Now, this also presents a great opportunity to ask your skeptical friends how they *know* that God is the way they say he is. Where do they get that information? Do they have access to the mind of God? If so, how? Most folks don't have an answer to that question. In fact, it will quickly become clear that most people's "god" is just a creation of their own minds. It is more about how they *want* God to be.

But this creates its own set of problems. If our God is just a reflection of our personal preferences and desires, then how could that God really be God? Aren't we really just making *ourselves* God? Or, as Timothy Keller has said, "If your god never disagrees with you, you might just be worshiping an idealized version of yourself."[3]

In contrast, Christians know what God is like by looking to the Scriptures. And thus it is very possible—in fact, very likely—that

we will find a God there who does not conform to our every prefer-
ence. We might even find a God who disagrees with us. Indeed, we
do find a God who is quite different from the one in most people's
minds. The God of the Bible is love but not *only* love. He is also
holy, righteous, and pure. He is not a one-dimensional God but a
God who is just *and* compassionate, wrathful *and* gracious, separate
from us *and* intimate with us.

We have examples in the Bible of people who meet God, and
usually their expectations are profoundly shattered. It's not a casual
"Hey, God, good to meet you!" but an awestruck wonder at God's
glory and holiness. The prophet Isaiah had just such an encounter.
He had a vision of God:

> I saw the Lord sitting upon a throne, high and lifted up; and the
> train of his robe filled the temple. . . . And one [seraph] called
> to another and said:
>
>> "Holy, holy, holy is the LORD of hosts;
>> the whole earth is full of his glory!"
>
> And the foundations of the thresholds shook at the voice of him
> who called, and the house was filled with smoke. (Isa. 6:1–4)

This is a terrifying scene. Smoke. Earthquakes. Angelic voices. All
of which point to the unspeakable, unmatchable glory of God.
This is why the book of Hebrews can say, "It is a fearful thing to
fall into the hands of the living God" (Heb. 10:31).

Here's the main point: if *this* God exists—the one who is "holy,
holy, holy"—then it makes a lot more sense to think that he might
judge sin after all.

Sinner, Meet Thyself

So the first step toward changing the way we think about hell is to come face-to-face with the true, living God. But there is also a second step. We also need to come face-to-face with *ourselves*. We need to realize that we are much bigger sinners than we could ever imagine. And, ironically, we see ourselves rightly only when we encounter the true and living God. When we compare ourselves to *his* perfect righteousness, then we begin to understand how far short we fall.

Isaiah learned this lesson the hard way. After he encountered God in all his glory, he basically fell apart: "And I said: 'Woe is me! For I am lost; for I am a man of unclean lips, and I dwell in the midst of a people of unclean lips; for my eyes have seen the King, the LORD of hosts!'" (Isa. 6:5). Essentially, Isaiah realized he was *dirty*—he called himself "unclean"—when in the presence of God's holiness. The brighter the light, the more dirt you will see. And keep in mind that Isaiah was a prophet, probably one of the holiest men around.

Unfortunately, this is not how people typically measure themselves. Most of us—if we're honest—spend the majority of our time comparing ourselves to those around us. We figure if we are just better than most people and haven't committed any serious crimes, then God is probably pretty pleased with us. Thus, we are certain that even if there is a hell, surely we will not find ourselves there. As Jonathan Edwards famously said, "Almost every natural man that hears of hell, flatters himself that he shall escape it."[4]

In other words, most people find hell unimaginable because they measure themselves by a standard that they can *already meet*.

But what if the standard was not easy to meet? What if the standard was God's perfect holiness, and what if we were corrupt, fallen sinners who violate God's law even more than we know? Jesus makes this reality plain when he says that we can break God's law not only in our actions but also in our *hearts*. Thus, Jesus can say, "Everyone who looks at a woman with lustful intent has already committed adultery with her in his heart" (Matt. 5:28).

Jesus's point is revolutionary. Holiness not only requires righteous actions (that's hard enough), it also requires a righteous heart. And that is a nearly impossible standard. On that standard, we sin a lot more than we realize. Indeed, one could say that our sins mount up—day after day, month after month, year after year—until they are a veritable Mount Everest. And most of us don't even know it.

Cosmic Treason

But if we are really going to see the seriousness of our sin, there is one more thing we need to consider. And this is something we tend to overlook. Typically, we think of sin as just breaking a rule (and there's a sense in which that is true). But we forget that sin is also breaking a *relationship*. Sin is when we take our deepest affections off the one who deserves them (God) and place them onto other things that do not.

Sin, then, is a form of cheating. It is cosmic treason. Or, in biblical language, it is *idolatry*. Remember the very first commandment: "You shall have no other gods before me" (Ex. 20:3).

You see, human beings are hardwired to be worshipers. That is how God made us. The issue is not *whether* we will worship. That's a given. The issue is the *object* of our worship. Who or what will we devote our life to? If we are not worshiping the one true God, then we will worship something else.

And when we commit idolatry, there are devastating consequences on ourselves and on others. On ourselves, our idols become harsh taskmasters, ruling our lives and even driving us to despair. If our idol is money, there is never enough of it. If it is sex, we realize it does not fulfill us. If it is "success" of some sort, then we eventually discover how pointless it all seems. Idols cannot bear the weight we place on them. They fail to live up to the divine status we give them.

Even so, people still refuse to give up their idols. The real tragedy comes when our idols are taken away from us (or someone tries to take them away from us), and our dependence on them is exposed. To keep our idols, we will lash out, fight back, destroy others—all because we have devoted our hearts to these false gods. It's not that different from the behavior of a drug addict. The very thing we love is the very thing that is destroying us. It's heartbreaking, really.

All the while, God offers himself as the one true God who can genuinely meet our needs, fulfill our desires, and satisfy our longings. And what do sinners do? We snub God, reject him, show contempt for his offers of mercy, and rush back to our idols. It is no surprise, then, that the Bible compares sinners to an unfaithful bride. Even though she lawfully and legally belongs to her husband, and even though he is kind, gracious, loving, and patient with her, she still runs off with other men.

That is what sin is like.

Nothing to See Here

So if God is more holy than we ever thought, and we are more sinful than we dared guess, then suddenly the doctrine of hell doesn't look so unimaginable. Suddenly it seems quite plausible that God might just judge our sin. If so, what can be done? Is there anything we can do to solve our sin problem?

Some will insist that there's not much to worry about here. Maybe God can just overlook our sins. Maybe God could just say,

"Don't worry about it, I forgive you. Nothing to see here." After all, isn't God in the forgiveness business? Isn't that his job?

But this line of reasoning ignores what we've just seen above. God cannot just "overlook" sins because to do so would compromise his holy character. It would make God an *unjust* judge. Think about it for a moment. What if a human judge was faced with an awful criminal in his courtroom—one who had committed unspeakable crimes—and just let him off the hook? It would be regarded as a travesty of justice.

Emma, when you were about ten years old, there was a tragic story in Charlotte of a little girl named Zahra Baker. I remember it well because you were the same age as Zahra at the time. The poor girl had a difficult life—she was diagnosed with cancer at a young age, which left her with an amputated leg and hearing problems. At one point, the girl went missing and a massive manhunt ensued as the police searched everywhere for her. Later it was discovered that her stepmother—who had repeatedly abused her over the years—murdered and dismembered the little girl. The crime captured the attention of the nation, especially the media in Charlotte. It was a gut-wrenching story. The stepmother was sentenced to nearly thirty years in prison.

But imagine if things had gone differently. Imagine if the judge had looked at Zahra Baker's stepmother and declared, "Hey, everyone makes mistakes. Not a big deal. All charges dropped." There would have been nationwide outrage over the injustice of it all. We all knew intuitively that this woman *had* to be punished. It was the right thing to do.

And if a human judge needs to punish sin in order to be just, how much more does a divine judge need to do so? If God just ignored people's sins, if he just overlooked them, then he would

himself be unjust. Indeed, he would not be a God worth following. As Miroslav Volf notes, "If God were *not angry* at injustice
and deception and did *not* make a final end to violence—that God
would not be worthy of worship."[5]

Here's the key point: God does not punish people in hell *despite* his goodness; he punishes people in hell *because* he is so *very
good*—more than we ever thought.

Apparently, Jesus agreed. If hell is the offensive doctrine people
claim that it is, they must reckon with the fact that Jesus plainly
embraced the doctrine of hell. For him it was a real place of eternal
torment where God executes his justice (Matt. 13:42; Mark 9:43;
Luke 16:23). Indeed, Jesus talked about hell much more than he
ever talked about heaven.

At this point, it might be worth asking your friends about their
concept of justice in the world. In their worldview, how will all
things eventually be "made right"? Or will they? If there's no final
judgment, then does all the awfulness of the world—child abuse,
genocide, oppression of the poor, sexual assault, and so forth—just
remain unaddressed and unresolved *forever*? What about the Hitlers
and the Stalins and the Ted Bundys? Or what about Zahra Baker's
stepmother? Will there *ever* be justice for them?

Your friends might begin to realize that they have a longing for
justice that their worldview cannot meet. Indeed, the ironic fact is
that a worldview *without* hell—their worldview—is the one that
is most unjust. As Vince Gilligan, the creator of the hit TV show
Breaking Bad, once admitted, "I feel some sort of need for biblical
atonement, or justice, or something. . . . I want to believe there's
a heaven. But I can't *not* believe there's a hell."[6]

Of course, your friends might concede this point and admit
that hell may exist after all. But, they will insist, it is only for really

awful people. And they will quickly exclude themselves: "That stepmother deserved justice, but my sins are not as bad as hers. I am not a murderer!" But that is exactly where the misconception lies. Our sins *are* that bad. Sin is not just a "mistake"; it is cosmic treason against the King of the universe. And Jesus said plainly that we can murder in our hearts: "Everyone who is angry with his brother . . . will be liable to the hell of fire" (Matt. 5:22).

Here's where we encounter one of the major problems with the way people view God's judgment on sin. They always view God's judgment as something that should fall on *other people's sins*—especially really bad people. The Bible says otherwise: "All have sinned and fall short of the glory of God" (Rom. 3:23).

Out, Damned Spot!

Some people may try another way to solve the problem of their sin. They may agree that God can't just overlook it, but they figure that maybe they can *make up for it*. If they can work really hard, commit themselves to holy living, and live a purer life, perhaps the good will outweigh the bad in the end. And perhaps that will be enough to cover up their sin.

Put another way, some people will try to address their sins by attempting some sort of *self-cleansing*. They try to wash away their own spots.

Back when I was a student at UNC years ago, a popular film was *The Mission*, starring Robert De Niro. The film tells the story of Captain Rodrigo Mendoza, a slave trader who murders his own brother in a fit of rage and finds himself in prison. Later, at the behest of a priest, Mendoza tries to make penance for his crimes by engaging in a grueling challenge to pull a heavy bundle of his old weapons up the mountain. The exhausting scene is the centerpiece of the film, highlighting one man's resolve to pay for the things he had done. And finally, after reaching the top of the mountain, he receives his forgiveness.

To be sure, the movie is powerful. And no doubt, many resonate with its themes. But does forgiveness really work that way? Can we really save ourselves by paying for our own sins? Time and again, the Bible makes it clear that God's forgiveness does *not* work like this. Our *future* law keeping cannot make up for *past* sins. Paul states plainly, "For all who rely on works of the law are under a curse" (Gal. 3:10). Even if we were perfect the rest of our lives (which we cannot be), that does not make up for the prior sins for which we are genuinely guilty. All our hard work—even our penance—cannot remove their stain.

The more accurate account of the way sin works is found in the story of Lady Macbeth in Shakespeare's *Macbeth*. Having orchestrated the murder of the king, she is haunted by her guilt. One night, while sleepwalking in the castle, she sees the blood of the murder on her hands and tries to wipe it away: "Out, damned spot!" But even in her dream, all her efforts cannot cleanse her hands. No penance can cover it. The blood remains.

So it is with us as sinners. Despite all our best efforts at self-improvement, our guilt cannot be washed away *by us*. That leaves only one option. It must be washed away *for us*.

Unfair in Our Favor

The above discussion helps us realize how dire our situation really is. Not only are we sinners rightly under God's wrath, but there's nothing that we can do about it. The only one who can do anything about it is (ironically) the very God we've offended.

And this should radically change the way we look at hell. Indeed, it flips everything on its head. Rather than be shocked that God would send anyone to hell, we should be shocked that he would save anyone at all. What should surprise us is not that God would judge sinners (that actually makes sense) but that he would save any of them.

Heaven, not hell, is the real mystery of Scripture. We should be blown away that there's a place like heaven, where a holy God and lost sinners can dwell together in peace and harmony.

And how is a place like heaven possible? It's possible—and you know this, Emma—because of what Jesus did on the cross. When he died on the cross, Jesus paid the penalty we deserve, absorbing all the wrath that is due to us. At the cross, God's justice is fully satisfied. Thus, he can be in a relationship with sinners without compromising his holiness.

Here's another way to look at it. On the cross, Jesus bore the punishments of hell we deserve. We don't have to face judgment in hell because Jesus, in effect, suffered the pangs of hell in our place. When we are united to him by faith, we receive the benefits of his saving work.

But here's the thing. God didn't *have* to send Jesus to die for sinners. God would be completely justified if he judged everyone and saved no one. If so, then this goes a long way toward answering the very common "man on the desert island" objection. The objection goes something like this: "If you have to believe in Jesus to be saved, then what about the man on the desert island who has never heard of Jesus? How can God send a person to hell for not believing in Jesus when he or she never had a chance to do so?"

But this objection misses the mark for a number of reasons. For one, people don't go to hell for "not believing in Jesus." They go to hell because they are rebellious sinners who have violated God's law. And even the man on the desert island knows God's law because it's written on his heart (Rom. 2:15). Second, the objection implies that God owes everyone a "chance" to be saved. Almost as if fairness demands it. But God does not owe salvation (or a chance at salvation) to anyone. Salvation is a *gift*. And gifts, by definition, are not obligatory—otherwise, they are not gifts.

Thus, just because God decides to save some people does not obligate him to save everyone.

During my time at UNC, I always made sure to grab a copy of the student newspaper, *The Daily Tarheel*, on the way to class every morning. But it wasn't for the articles. It was for my all-time favorite comic strip, *Calvin and Hobbes*. It's a comic about a precocious six-year-old boy named Calvin and his stuffed tiger, Hobbes (who's alive in Calvin's imagination). In one particular installment, Calvin is complaining to his father about how something is unfair. His father gives a typical response: "The world isn't fair." Calvin's reply is priceless: "I know, but why isn't it ever unfair *in my favor?*"

That pretty well captures God's grace. If God is unfair to sinners at all, then we might say he's unfair *in our favor*. He saves us when we don't deserve it.

———

Emma, the idea of God's judgment and an eternal hell is a hard doctrine to grasp. And it will be tempting to downplay it, minimize it, or even do away with it altogether. But as we have seen above, there is a biblical logic to the doctrine. Once you understand who God really is (he is holy) and who we really are (we are sinful), then hell is not the unthinkable doctrine that it seems.

But we must keep the doctrine of hell for another reason. If we lose hell, we lose the gospel. We might think we make God more loving by diminishing the doctrine of hell. But ironically, it turns out that the opposite is the case. To diminish hell is to diminish what Christ did for us on the cross. It actually makes God *less* loving because it makes what Christ did on the cross less significant.

Thus, believe it or not, hell becomes the key to unlocking God's vast, unfathomable *love*. "God shows his love for us in that while we were still sinners, Christ died for us" (Rom. 5:8).

Love,

Dad

There Is So Much Suffering in the World—How Could a Good God Allow Such Evil?

Without God . . . everything is permitted.
FYODOR DOSTOEVSKY, *THE BROTHERS KARAMAZOV*

Dearest Emma,

In September 2001, our family had just moved back from Scotland. You were a tiny baby, not even one year old. One morning, your mom called out to me from the other room: "A plane just hit the World Trade Center!" I rushed to the television and watched in horror as one of the towers burned. Then, soon after, I watched as a second plane crashed into the other tower. Before it would all be over, the United States would lose nearly three thousand of its own citizens to terrorist attacks. The world would never be the same.

As I looked at you in your crib, you were still asleep. I was thankful you did not have to experience the devastation of that day, nor the immediate aftermath. And ever since, you have enjoyed a relatively safe and prosperous life, at least compared to most people in the world. One of the blessings of being young is that you have had little opportunity to experience (or watch others experience) serious suffering. Overall, the world seems like a great place. And there's nothing wrong with that. It's a blessing from God.

But you are quickly discovering that college exposes you to a whole new—and sometimes much darker—world. And when you learn more about what is happening around the globe, you will see that the world is not always such a great place. In many places, suffering is not the exception but the rule. Whether because of wars, economic crises, food shortages, or lack of health care, many people are seriously hurting on a daily basis.

Even more, you are learning in your classes about the various forms of suffering that have happened *historically*. Some of this suffering was due to natural disasters, like floods, volcanoes, or the spread of disease. In the Middle Ages, the black death is estimated to have killed as much as 50 percent of Europe's population in just a four-year period—possibly as many as two hundred million people. Beyond this are the numerous atrocities committed over the years that make the devastation of 9/11 seem tiny by comparison. Hitler killed six million Jews. Some have estimated that Stalin killed up to twenty million of his own people. And Mao Tse-tung may have been responsible for the deaths of forty-five million people.

In addition, you will make new friends at UNC and learn of their own stories of suffering. While they may not be comparable to the suffering under Nazi Germany, they are very painful for those who've endured them. Some have lost loved ones. Some have come from broken homes. Some have been abused. Some have suffered from serious illness. The stories will be hard to hear. In such cases, you will want to walk alongside those who suffer—loving them, praying for them, and hurting with them. While you can never fully understand what they are going through, at least you can be there for them.

But as you are exposed to more and more suffering, you will be faced with questions about more than just how to care for people. You are going to start asking some foundational *intellectual* questions. If God is a good God, then why doesn't he just stop all this suffering? Is he not *able* to stop it? Or does he not *want* to? Neither option seems like a good one. On top of this you will learn that all this suffering has been one of the primary reasons people reject Christianity. Indeed, the "problem of evil," as it is called, has been used as one of the foremost arguments for atheism.

So it is critical that we think through these important questions. As we do so, however, an essential yet simple reminder is in order: *we are not God.* I know that's obvious, but it is worth saying explicitly. It means we should not be surprised if there are things about God's ways that we don't fully understand. Some people demand to understand *everything* before they are willing to assent to the existence (or goodness) of God. But that is an unreasonable standard. These issues are very complex, and we are finite, fallen people. In the end, we may not have all the answers we wish for. But we can still trust in the Lord and trust that he knows best.

Paul expressed this same posture of humility when he dealt with his own difficult questions about God:

Oh, the depth of the riches and wisdom and knowledge of God! How unsearchable are his judgments and how inscrutable his ways!

"For who has known the mind of the Lord,
  or who has been his counselor?" (Rom. 11:33–34)

And then, even though he doesn't understand everything, Paul can still praise the Lord in the very next sentence: "For from him and through him and to him are all things. To him be glory forever. Amen" (Rom. 11:36).

So What's the Problem Exactly?

We should begin by defining the problem of evil more specifically. What *exactly* is the argument that atheists are making? Generally speaking, it runs as follows:

1. If God were all-good, then he would *want* to prevent all evil.
2. If God were all-powerful, then he would be *able* to prevent all evil.
3. Evil exists.
4. Therefore, an all-good and all-powerful God cannot exist.

In his book *The Problem of Pain*, C. S. Lewis puts the claim this way:

> If God were good, He would wish to make His creatures perfectly happy, and if God were almighty He would be able to do what He wished. But the creatures are not happy. Therefore, God lacks either goodness, or power, or both.

At first glance, that argument seems pretty compelling. It might appear as if the Christian concept of God has real problems. But as you know, things are never that cut-and-dried. Christians have been aware of this issue from the very beginning and have offered a number of solutions over the years.

Of course, that doesn't mean that all the attempted solutions are good ones. Some Christians have tried to solve the problem of evil by conceding that God is not all-powerful after all. Maybe God is just as upset about the state of the world as we are. He wants to change it but lacks full control over all the moving parts. Some used this approach to deal with the tragedy of 9/11. God was just not able to stop it.

But even a basic knowledge of Scripture shows that this does not fit at all with the Christian God. The God of the Bible is not weak, impotent, and incapable of stopping evil. On the contrary, God says, "Behold, I am the LORD, the God of all flesh. Is anything too hard for me?" (Jer. 32:27). To argue that God is not all-powerful may technically solve the problem of evil, but one is left with something other than the Christian God.

Another attempted solution to the problem of evil is known as the "free-will defense." According to this view, God is all-powerful, but he *voluntarily* restricts his power so as not to interfere with the free decisions of human beings. God does this so that humans love him by choice, not out of coercion. But there is a price to pay for such freedom. Humans can reject God and commit acts of evil—which is what they've done. Such an outcome is not God's fault. The blame lies with humans.

Now, the free-will defense is certainly a better option than denying that God is all-powerful. But it runs into its own set of problems. Most fundamentally, the Bible makes it clear that God *does* control the "free" actions of men! He raises up human armies (Josh. 11:20; Hab. 1:6), steers the hearts of kings (Ezra 6:22; Prov. 21:1), and even hardens people's hearts (Deut. 2:30; Rom. 9:18). Moreover, Paul plainly states that God "works *all things* according to the counsel of his will" (Eph. 1:11), which must certainly include human decisions. While the relationship between God's sovereignty and human responsibility is complex (and even mysterious), there is no indication that God lacks control over such a huge part of the created world.

A Better Solution

Although these attempted solutions are problematic, there is a better option. When we look closer at the individual parts of the argument above, we can see that there is a serious problem with premise 1: "If God were all-good, then he would want to prevent all evil." That premise works only if something else is true, namely, that God has *no good reason* for allowing evil. But what if God *does* have a good reason for allowing evil? If he does, then premise 1 simply doesn't work. If God does have a good reason, then he would *not* want to prevent evil in every circumstance.

To illustrate, imagine if we used a similar argument for parents: good parents would never let their child feel pain; otherwise, they must not be good. Such a principle holds only if parents have *no good reason* for allowing their child to feel pain. But we can imagine many good reasons why a parent might allow pain. If the child has an intestinal blockage, the parents would be quite willing to allow the pain of emergency surgery. If a child has a propensity to run into the street, the parents might employ some form of discipline (i.e., pain!) that would motivate the child to stay near mom and dad. If a child has a cavity, a parent would be quite ready to let the child endure the pain of a filling. In such cases, parents can be good and can allow pain *at the same time.*

No doubt, your skeptical friend will object to this line of reasoning. She might say, "Yeah, but *God* could not possibly have a good reason for allowing evil." But how does your friend know this? Is your classmate in an intellectual position to know what is possible or impossible in the universe? Can she know all the options pertaining to reasons why God might allow evil? In essence, she is arguing, "Since I *personally* can see no reason, there can't be a reason." But that is just a bad argument. God may have many good reasons for allowing evil that we are simply unaware of.

Your friend's line of reasoning would be the equivalent of me going up to the physics lab of MIT—which houses some of the smartest scientists on the planet—and telling them that there's no way their experiment will work because *I personally don't get it*. But how am I in a position to know this? What do I know about advanced physics? Nothing! Or, as another example, it would be like me watching the world chess championship and telling Magnus Carlsen (the reigning champ) that he's definitely stuck because *I personally don't see a viable move*. But given how little I know about chess (virtually nothing), that is not a very good argument. How would I know what moves are left?

Here's the point: Just because we don't know all the reasons God has for allowing evil, that doesn't mean he does not (or could not) have them. And unless the skeptic can *prove* that God could not possibly have a good reason for allowing evil—which is impossible—then his argument falls apart.

Of course, some skeptics will not be deterred. Despite not having a good argument, they will just *insist* that God could not have a good reason for allowing evil. It just can't be so! It reminds me of the dramatic courtroom scene in the film *A Few Good Men*, in which the assisting attorney JoAnne Galloway (played by Demi Moore) does something similar. Realizing that they were losing the actual argument, she bursts forth with an emotional plea: "Your honor, we renew our objection!" When she gets no traction with the judge, she can only insist further: "Sir, the defense *strenuously* objects!" She substituted an emotional declaration for an actual argument. And the whole courtroom could see it.

This actually reveals something about skeptics that is often overlooked, namely, that they take a blind leap of faith. They will insist on believing something even with no reason to do so.

God's Purposes for Evil

We are arguing here that God would not stop evil in every instance if he had a good reason for allowing it. So what would be some of these good reasons? Does the Bible hint at any of them? Yes, let me mention just a few.

First, God uses suffering to make us more Christlike. What shapes our character most effectively is not our pleasure but our pain. It teaches us to deny ourselves and depend more on God, and it even generates sympathy toward others. Peter reminds us, "You have been grieved by various trials, so that the tested genuineness of your faith—more precious than gold that perishes though it is tested by fire—may be found to result in praise and glory and honor at the revelation of Jesus Christ" (1 Pet. 1:6–7). Even Jesus himself was made "perfect through suffering" (Heb. 2:10).

Second, God often uses suffering as a form of divine judgment. Throughout the Bible, it is clear that God uses a range of calamities—from natural disasters, to diseases, to foreign armies—to judge people for their sins. The classic example, of course, is Noah's flood. Although the people of earth would have been unaware of the reason for the flood, it is clear that God sent it because "the wickedness of man was great in the earth" (Gen. 6:5). Of course, this does not mean that all suffering is directly related to a person's sin, but sometimes it is.

Third, and perhaps most importantly, God uses suffering as an opportunity to display his glory in redemption. Without evil in the world, we would not be able to experience (and praise God for) his salvation, mercy, and grace. On a very basic level, we can see this principle in the story of the man born blind. Jesus is very clear that he wasn't born blind because he sinned or because his parents sinned but "that the works of God might be displayed in him" (John 9:3). Thus, the suffering of the world provides an opportunity for a greater good, namely, the magnification of God as Redeemer.

As I mentioned before, I loved reading *The Lord of the Rings* aloud to you and John and Kate when you were younger. The three of you would listen closely, hanging on every word. It allowed us to experience that great epic together—a tale filled with much darkness, sorrow, and suffering. But at the end of the story, after the ring has been destroyed and the forces of darkness have been defeated, the characters experience the most profound and unexpected joy. A key scene with Sam and Gandalf captures this so well:

> But Sam lay back, and stared with open mouth, and for a moment, between bewilderment and great joy, he could not answer. At last he gasped: "Gandalf! I thought you were dead! But then I thought I was dead myself. Is everything sad going to come untrue? What's happened to the world?"
>
> "A great Shadow has departed," said Gandalf, and then he laughed, and the sound was like music, or like water in a parched land; and as he listened the thought came to Sam that he had not heard laughter, the pure sound of merriment, for days upon days without count. It fell upon his ears like the echo of all the joys he had ever known. But he himself burst into tears. Then as sweet rain will pass down a wind of spring and the sun will shine out the clearer, his tears ceased, and his laughter welled up, and laughing he sprang from his bed.

"How do I feel?" he cried. "Well, I don't know how to say it. I feel, I feel"—he waved his arms in the air—"I feel like spring after winter, and sun on the leaves; and like trumpets and harps and all the songs I have ever heard!"[1]

Indeed, the joy Sam experienced could never have been so deep without all the suffering they had experienced. You might even say that the evil was used to bring about a greater good.

To be clear, these are just three ways that God uses suffering for his purposes and are not meant to explain *every* instance of evil in the world. Indeed, God may have many good reasons for the suffering he allows even if he does not share those reasons with us. As I mentioned above, we should not expect to understand everything about God's ways. On the contrary, as fallen finite human beings, we should even expect *not* to understand.

In fact, the Bible is filled with instances in which God has ordained suffering for a good purpose *even though that purpose is not revealed at the time.* The classic example is the story of Joseph. Betrayed by his own brothers and sold into slavery, Joseph experienced immense suffering. And no doubt, it might have seemed meaningless and purposeless to Joseph. But God revealed later that it had a good purpose, namely, to get Joseph to Egypt so that he could later rescue his family members from a coming famine. And why was that so important? Because from that family would come the future Messiah, the Savior of the world. This allowed Joseph to say to his brothers, "You meant evil against me, but God meant it for good, to bring it about that many people should be kept alive" (Gen. 50:20). Here, then, is a classic example of God allowing evil to bring about a greater good even though he did not reveal his reasons until later.

But there is an even better example of God using evil to bring about a greater good. And that is Jesus's death on the cross. There is no doubt that the cross accomplishes what is arguably the greatest good in the world, the redemption of sinners. Indeed, the cross accomplishes a good that might have seemed impossible—bringing peace between a holy God and sinful people. And yet, God accomplishes this good result *through various sorts of evil and suffering.* Jesus was falsely accused, given a sham of a trial, beaten and tortured, and publicly executed by the Romans. All these evils were done according to what God's "plan had predestined to take place" (Acts 4:28). Once again, God used evil—in this case, even the murder of the Son of God—to bring about a greater good.

Of course, as Jesus endured these great acts of evil, God's ultimate good purpose would not yet have been clear. In fact, Jesus's own disciples seemed to despair at his death, hiding in the upper room and fearing for their lives. They might have assumed that God, if he allowed his own Son to die, must not really be sovereign after all. Moreover, they might have assumed that God could not possibly have a good reason for letting such a tragedy happen. They might even have assumed that God was not really good. But later, after the resurrection, all those assumptions would be proved wrong. God *did* have a good reason for allowing all that suffering, even though the disciples did not understand it at the time.

So again, just because we don't know what good reasons God might have for allowing suffering, that doesn't mean those reasons don't (or can't) exist. If God can take the greatest evil in the world (the death of his Son) and use it for good, could he not also do that for all the other evils in the world? We need to remember the words of Paul: "How unsearchable are his judgments and how inscrutable his ways!" (Rom. 11:33).

Who Really Has a Problem Explaining Evil?

At this point, it is clear that the problem of evil—though difficult and even troubling—does not provide a good reason to reject the God of Christianity. We have argued that God could (and does) have good reasons for allowing evil even if he does not fully share what those reasons are.

But we don't want to stop here. It's not just the Christian who has to account for evil in the universe. Every worldview has to offer an explanation for evil. No one gets a free pass. And this is particularly true for atheists because the problem of evil is one of the main reasons *they* have rejected the existence of God. In other words, most atheists are not merely pointing out an internal problem in the Christian worldview; rather they are appealing to all the evil in the universe as justification for their *own* worldview.

Okay, fair enough. But that means the atheist has to explain where good and evil come from. Or, even more to the point, the atheist has to explain how one knows good and evil when he sees it. And as observed in one of my prior letters to you, this is a major problem for atheism. After all, most atheists believe in material-ism—the idea that the universe is made up of only matter and energy. There are no gods, angels, or spiritual beings. The universe is just filled with rocks, trees, molecules, stars, black holes, and so on. Thus, everything can be explained by science. The laws of physics are the only laws that matter.

But how then does the atheist explain the existence of "evil"? Or, even more, how does she explain the existence of "good"? In a materialistic universe, on what basis could we declare one action "evil" and another action "good"? Physics can explain how things behave, but it cannot explain how they *ought* to behave. If the universe is the result of randomness and chance, there's no reason to think things ought to be one way as opposed to another. Things just are. In an atheistic world, there is no *ought*.

Many atheists, then, find themselves in a bit of an intellectual pickle. They have appealed to the reality of evil in the world as a basis to object to God's existence.[2] But without God's existence, there's no reason to think that evil (or good) is real.

Curiously, this is precisely the dilemma that led C. S. Lewis to abandon his atheism and turn to Christianity. Lewis writes,

> My argument against God was that the universe seemed so cruel and unjust. But how had I got this idea of *just* and *unjust*? A man does not call a line crooked unless he has some idea of a straight line. What was I comparing the universe to when I called it unjust? . . . Of course, I could have given up my idea of justice by saying it was nothing but a private idea of my own. But if I did that, then my argument against God collapsed too—for the argument depended on saying that the world was really unjust, not simply that it did not happen to please my private fancies.[3]

Even modern atheists have come to feel the weight of what Lewis experienced. Some are realizing that their atheism is really an "all or nothing" endeavor. Either God exists and there's good and evil in the world, or God doesn't exist and there's no good and evil in the world. It's one or the other. The real question is whether they have the fortitude to live out what they claim to believe. As Fyodor Dostoevsky once wrote in *The Brothers Karamazov*, "Without God . . . everything is permitted."[4]

In the end, the problem of evil is very real. But it is more of a problem for the atheist than it is for the Christian.

———

Sometimes the world is a dark place. There is real suffering all around us. And some people use this suffering as a reason to reject God. But I hope this letter helps you see that the opposite should be the case. The existence of evil should make us not reject God but embrace him. The existence of a good God is the only foundation we have for distinguishing between good and evil.

On top of this, God is the only one who has done anything to solve the problem of evil. Someday, he will set all things right, and evil will be vanquished forever: "He will wipe away every tear from their eyes, and death shall be no more, neither shall there be mourning, nor crying, nor pain anymore, for the former things have passed away" (Rev. 21:4).

Love,

Dad

8

Science Seems Like It Can Explain Everything in the Universe— Do We Really Need to Believe in God?

There is no heaven or afterlife . . . ; that is a
fairy story for people afraid of the dark.
STEPHEN HAWKING

Dearest Emma,

One thing I know you are excited about is your new major: medicine. You've always had a desire to help people in need, and being a doctor or a nurse is a great way to do that. But that is not an easy field of study. Science courses—from biochemistry to anatomy to microbiology—will dominate your studies. And you may begin to wonder whether Christianity fits with science—or, more to the point, whether the Bible is compatible with what you are learning in class. And what do you do if they seem to conflict? Do you abandon science? Or do you abandon the Bible?

In 2016, a revealing study about science and religion was released.[1] In many ways, it told us what we sort of already knew: scientists—at least in the United States—are much *less* religious than the general population. Indeed, 33 percent of the general US population attends weekly religious services, whereas only 11 percent of scientists do—a disparity of more than two to one. It almost seems as if the more you know about science, the less you need God.

Of course, studies like this one tap into the long-standing perception that science is at war with religion, perhaps especially the Christian religion. Ever since the church contested Galileo's finding that the earth revolved around the sun, it seems like science and Christianity have been locked in a never-ending battle over people's souls. And like any war, people feel like they eventually have to pick a side.

The perceived science-religion battle is exacerbated by some who are stoking the fires of the conflict. It's almost as if they *want* science and religion to be at odds. In his provocative book *The God Delusion*, the popular atheist and evolutionary scientist Richard Dawkins basically argues that the more people embrace science, the less they will embrace God—as if the two are mutually exclusive.[2] Hostile comments about religion from leading scientists such as Stephen Hawking also play a role: "There is no heaven or afterlife . . . ; that is a fairy story for people afraid of the dark."[3]

But is there *really* a war between science and Christianity? Not at all. Let me use this letter to dispel the myth that Christianity is antiscience. My hope is that you will see that the true findings of science do not present a reason to reject Christianity but actually present many reasons to accept it.

Christianity's (Surprisingly) Scientific Heritage

If you listened only to the rhetoric of our modern day, you would get the impression that no respectable scientist would be a Christian. Largely forgotten, however, is the great history of scientists who were Christians (or at least committed theists) and saw no conflict between their vocation and their faith. Indeed, few seem to remember that the scientific method itself was the result, at least in large part, of the work of committed Christians such as Roger Bacon and William of Ockham.[4] And they were followed by a whole line of scientists—really the "founding fathers" of science—who embraced a Christian/theistic worldview. Examples include Johannes Kepler, Robert Boyle, Blaise Pascal, Isaac Newton, and Gregor Mendel. We should also remember that even Galileo—despite his conflict with the Catholic church—considered himself a Christian.

In the modern day, we still find many committed Christians in the scientific world. We can point to the likes of Francis Collins, director of the National Institutes of Health and head of the Human Genome Project, and John Lennox, professor of mathematics at the University of Oxford. In her recent book *Confronting Christianity*, Rebecca McLaughlin even provides an impressive list of *current* professors at MIT who are professing Christians, ranging across fields from physics to chemistry and beyond.[5] Even more, Lennox points out that over 60 percent of the Nobel Prize winners between 1900 and 2000 identified themselves as Christians.[6]

This positive connection between Christianity and science should not be surprising given that Christianity provides a great *motivation* to do science. Historically, Christians have viewed the scientific enterprise as a way to uncover and explore what God did when he created the world. As Kepler himself said, "The chief aim of all investigations of the external world should be to discover the rational order which has been imposed on it by God."[7]

Emma, when you were a child, we used to take you and your siblings to the annual Easter egg hunt at a local park. There were thousands of eggs spread across the park, and the organizers of the event had hidden a "golden ticket" inside a few of them. The ticket could be exchanged for prizes, candy, and other fun items. As soon as the horn blew, you would take off at a full sprint, eager to explore and discover. Why? Because you knew that someone had placed a treasure out there just waiting to be found. It's kind of like that with Christians and science. We have a great motivation for scientific pursuits because we know an intelligent person has created this universe. And we get to discover all the wonders and treasures that he has put there.

So what should we make of the statistics in the 2016 study discussed above that scientists are much less likely to be religious? Interestingly, if you dive deeper into the numbers, that trend holds mainly in the West, particularly in the United States and Great Britain. When other regions are considered—like Taiwan, Turkey, and India—the religious disparity between scientists and the general population largely disappears. What does that mean? It means that the perceived conflict between science and religion is a largely Western (not to mention, recent) phenomenon.

We should also consider the limitation of such statistical studies. They may describe what scientists believe, but they don't show us *why* they believe it. Just because most scientists are nonreligious, that does not mean that they are nonreligious *because of science*. People's religious beliefs are influenced by all sorts of factors that these studies don't reveal—family background, personal experience, cultural influence, education. So we must be careful not to blame science itself for people's lack of religious commitment. Many scientists may have brought their religious skepticism *to* science rather than deriving it *from* science.

Does Christianity Need Science? Or Does Science Need Christianity?

There's yet another reason that science and Christianity are not (or should not be) at war, namely, that science actually *needs* Christianity in order to work. Now, that might sound like an odd thing to say, so let me explain. Most people never stop to think about it, but the entire scientific enterprise is actually built on certain *philosophical* principles—principles that themselves aren't drawn from science. Put differently, science could not function properly on just any worldview. It needs a worldview in which the universe operates in an orderly, predictable, uniform fashion—what scientists call the *uniformity of nature.*

Why is the uniformity of nature so important? It's important because, otherwise, scientific experiments have no validity. Imagine, for example, that you do an experiment to determine the boiling point of water, and you discover that it boils at 212°F. Normally, scientists extrapolate from this observation that tomorrow (given the same conditions), water will also boil at 212°F. But that extrapolation works only if one assumes the uniformity of nature—that is, if one assumes that the future will be like the past. If one did *not* assume the uniformity of nature, then one would have to admit that water tomorrow might just boil at a very different temperature, maybe 57°F. And the day after that it might boil at, say, 1026°F! So scientists must assume the uniformity of nature, or they could never reach any *conclusions* from experimentation.

And it's not just science that requires a belief in the uniformity of nature. Even our day-to-day lives assume that the world works in a predictable, orderly fashion. For example, when we go to sleep at night, we don't strap ourselves to our beds, worried that gravity might just randomly stop in the middle of the night and that we might float up and hit the ceiling. No, we assume that the universe will continue to operate like it always has. We assume that the future will be like the past and that gravity will work again tonight.

So here's the key question: Which worldview provides a basis for affirming the uniformity of nature? Put another way, which worldview provides a reason to think that *the future will be like the past*? Well, certainly not the atheistic-evolutionary worldview! If all the universe is random and unpredictable—beholden only to chance—then we have no reason to affirm the uniformity of nature and thus no reason to think that science would work at all. The atheist is free to assume it, but he does so without any basis. It is effectively a *blind leap of faith*.

Of course, the atheist will object at this point by saying something like "We don't need God to believe in the uniformity of nature. We believe the future will be like the past because every other time we've done so, it has worked. We believe it based on past experience." But this misses the point entirely. The fundamental question is *why past experience should be a reliable guide for the future*. Pointing to the past simply begs the question. Therefore, we have to have some *other* reason (besides the past) to affirm the uniformity of nature.

Indeed, this is precisely why philosophers have argued that only a Christian worldview can supply a reasonable basis for the uniformity of nature.[8] God as the Creator, Sustainer, and Upholder of the universe gives us a solid reason to think that the future will work like the past—the very thing an atheistic worldview does not provide.

If so, then we are faced with a rather ironic situation. Far from being a hindrance to science, belief in God is the very thing that makes science possible in the first place! Christianity doesn't need science; science needs Christianity.[9]

Separating Fact from Theory

Amid all the rhetoric over Christianity versus science, there is often a failure to distinguish carefully between opposition to a particular scientific theory and opposition to science itself. When it comes to science itself—a *method* of investigation that values observation of the natural world, developing hypotheses, and testing those hypotheses through experimentation—Christians have no quarrel. We are quite eager to participate and make contributions.

This has to be distinguished, however, from what Christians think about particular *theories* that happen to be prominent in the modern day, such as continental drift, geological uniformitarianism, or biological evolution. One can disagree with a particular theory without being antiscience.

Of course, many in the scientific community—especially those who insist that science is at odds with religion—disagree. They insist that something like evolution is not a theory but a *fact*. And therefore, to disagree with a well-established scientific fact makes one a religious fundamentalist who is disqualified from the scientific guild. To deny evolution has become the equivalent of being a flat-earther. As Richard Dawkins once said, "It is absolutely safe to say that if you meet somebody who claims not to believe in evolution, that person is ignorant, stupid or insane."[10]

But there are a number of problems with this approach. For one, establishing a hard "orthodoxy" in the guild of science to which everyone must conform (or else) is precisely the opposite of what science should encourage. The ideals of science include the freedom to question and challenge the standard theories and the freedom to go wherever the evidence takes you. Unfortunately, it seems like the modern scientific guild is often more interested in enforcing the evolutionary paradigm than allowing the freedom to ask difficult questions.

Indeed, one might even say that Darwinists sometimes function like the fundamentalists they often criticize. Darwinism has become its own religion.

The religious nature of evolution has been recently observed by the accomplished Yale professor David Gelernter. Having publicly come out that he is opposed to Darwinian evolution, Gelernter describes the modern field of science as having a decided "ideological bent" that tolerates no dissent: "You take your life in your hands to challenge it [evolution] intellectually. They will destroy you if you challenge it."[11] In other words, there is no academic freedom in this area. He states, "Darwinism is no longer just a scientific theory but the basis of a worldview, and an emergency replacement religion for the many troubled souls who need one."[12]

Second, such a top-down enforcement of evolutionary theory gives the impression that the scientific method produces conclusions with *absolute certainty*. Indeed, if Darwinism is a new religion, then here's its own doctrine of infallibility. But as I discussed in my first letter, science is not a bulletproof methodology that always yields true results. Science works through existing "paradigms" that determine how the facts are identified, sorted, and interpreted. Moreover, scientists themselves are fallible, fallen, and, yes, biased creatures who bring their own slants to their scientific research. So it is very possible that science can reach mistaken conclusions. Indeed, one might even say that the history of science is in many ways the history of wrong conclusions that have been overturned at a later point. And don't forget that each of these overturned theories was at one point regarded as established fact.

As an example, consider Ernst Haeckel's famous theory of *embryonic recapitulation*. His theory suggested that when the human embryo develops in the womb, it repeats the various stages of our evolutionary history. At one point the human embryo has gills, then later it forms a tail, and finally it becomes a full human. Thus, he argued, you can "see" our evolutionary history played out in the womb. For generations, Haeckel's theory was widely promulgated in scientific textbooks as fact. The theory (or parts of it) even remained in some textbooks into the 1990s. The problem with Haeckel's theory is that it turned out to be flat-out wrong. Now scientists know that the human embryo does not have "gills" or a "tail" at all.

Third, and perhaps most importantly, the insistence that evolution is an indisputable fact simply overlooks *serious scientific problems* with the theory. One does not need to believe the Bible to have a reason to doubt evolution. Science itself provides many good reasons. While we lack space to explore these problems here, they include questions about the origins of the first living cell, how order can increase in the face of the second law of thermodynamics, and the systemic gaps in the fossil record.[13] But there is one problem that stands out among the rest: the *origin of new genetic information*.

If you think about it, evolution requires massive structural changes within organisms. Organisms that are invertebrates (eventually) become vertebrates. Organisms without wings (eventually) get wings. Organisms without eyes (eventually) get eyes. Each one of these new structural features—wings, eyes, skeletons—requires massive amounts of new genetic information. This genetic information (stored in the DNA) contains the "assembly instructions" for how an organism is built.

But that raises an enormous question for the evolutionary theory. How does an organism get *new* genetic information? How does an organism that does not have "assembly instructions" for wings get those instructions? Evolutionary biologists have argued that the solution lies in random mutations in the genetic code. Perhaps, over billions of years, some mutations might have changed the genetic code in positive ways—ways that could have produced new physical features in an organism.

Recent advances in molecular biology, however, have shown that random mutations just don't have this creative ability. There is just not time to randomly assemble various genetic sequences in hopes of producing a new functional protein. Stephen Meyer describes the problem:

> It turns out that it is extremely difficult to assemble new genes or proteins by the random mutation and natural selection process because of the sheer number of possible sequences that must be searched by mutations in the available time.[14]

To try to acquire new genetic information this way, argues Meyer, is like a thief trying to guess the numerical combination of a bike lock. But rather than the standard four-digit bike lock, imagine if the lock were made up of ten digits. That is a lock with *ten billion* possible combinations and only one combination that actually works! A bike thief would be unlikely to find the right combination even he spent his whole life trying.

This reason alone—a *scientific* reason—is why many consider evolution to be an untenable theory. It just doesn't have a plausible mechanism for producing the vast amount of genetic information that would have been needed to produce new organisms.

So What Role Does the Bible Play?

Looming in the background of all these discussions is the question of what role (if any) the Bible should play in the scientific enterprise. Of course, for non-Christian scientists, it seems ridiculous to even ask such a question. The Bible should certainly *not* play a role, they would argue, nor should any other religious book. Science is about empirical evidence, not religion.

But it's not that simple for Christians. If the Bible is really God's word—as Christians have historically believed—then how could we ignore its own descriptions about the history of the world? Shouldn't those texts play *some* role in shaping our understanding of the origins of the universe?

Our answer to these questions depends, of course, on how we interpret the early chapters of Genesis—a long-standing point of disagreement among Christians. Some Christians argue that these chapters are largely poetic and are not to be taken as a historical account of the creation of the world. The Bible is not a scientific textbook, we are told. Christians who hold this position would be more open to believing that God might even have used a process like evolution to create the world.

Now, it is certainly true that the Bible is not a scientific textbook. It doesn't tell us how to build bridges or send a rover to Mars. But does that mean it has *no* bearing on our scientific endeavors? Other Christians have pushed back against this notion, arguing that the early chapters of Genesis are written in a style consistent with historical narrative, not poetry. Moreover, it seems that many New Testament figures, including Jesus himself, viewed Genesis as straightforward history. Adam and Eve were real historical figures, not symbols or a myth (Matt. 19:4–6; Rom. 5:12–21; 1 Tim. 2:13–14).

For those who take Genesis this way—as a historical book— accepting the theory of evolution becomes much more difficult. For one, Adam was directly and specially created by God (Gen. 2:7), ruling out that he evolved from some earlier race of hominids. Moreover, Genesis repeatedly states that animals were created "according to their kind"—a phrase that, at least on first view, seems to suggest that animals were created in distinct groups and are not merely the product of an earlier (and more primitive) life-form.

My purpose here is not to resolve this long-standing debate over the early chapters of Genesis. I simply want to point out that it is not unreasonable to think that Genesis, if it is real history, should play a role in the scientific endeavors of Christians. Thus, Christians may reject a theory like evolution on scientific grounds. But they may also reject it on biblical-theological grounds. And there's nothing illegitimate about that.

An example might help. Imagine for a moment that scientists were able to examine the first man, Adam, five minutes after he was directly created by God from the dust of the ground. If they did a thorough examination of Adam—measuring height, weight, physical development, and so on—they might conclude that Adam was something like twenty-five years old. Although their conclusions would be reasonable, even scientific, they would also be wrong. Adam would be only five minutes old. To get the right conclusions, they would need to *listen to God* regarding how he made Adam. Once they had done that, they could interpret the data properly.

Now, you might wonder, "If the Bible can challenge our interpretation of the natural world, is there ever a time when the natural world can challenge our understanding of the Bible?" Of course! Returning to the story of Galileo, many in his day understood certain biblical passages to mean that the sun moved and not the earth. Take, for example, Psalm 104:5:

> He set the earth on its foundations,
>   so that it should never be moved.

Obviously, Galileo's scientific work showed that this passage cannot be understood as ruling out the planetary motion of the earth. The interpretation of the passage that was popular in Galileo's day needed to be adjusted.

Here's the point: There is a complex relationship between the Bible and science that goes in both directions. And we cannot resolve all those complexities here. But we don't want to make the mistake of taking the Bible out of the discussion, as if it were irrelevant to the way we do science. No, God gave us his word to guide us in our understanding of the world. And that includes, among many things, the field of science.

———

The relationship between science and Christianity is a difficult topic. It will take years of reflection and study—of both Scripture and science—in order to reach some conclusions about the particulars. But the big picture is not in doubt. If God made this world, then believers can vigorously and optimistically pursue scientific studies for his glory. Indeed, as we discussed above, Christianity actually provides the philosophical soil in which science grows and prospers.

My prayer is that your scientific studies will allow you to say with the psalmist,

The heavens declare the glory of God,
  and the sky above proclaims his handiwork. (Ps. 19:1)

Love,

Dad

9

I'm Finding It Harder to Believe in Events Like the Resurrection— How Can I Believe in Miracles If I've Never Seen One?

"This is impossible," said Alice.
"Only if you believe it is," replied the Mad Hatter.
LEWIS CARROLL, *ALICE IN WONDERLAND*

Dearest Emma,

I can still remember the first time I read the Easter story to you as a small child. In our daily devotionals, we were working our way through the story of Jesus's life and came to the story of his crucifixion. As you heard the story, you wept profusely, saddened and heartbroken over the death of Jesus. But as we came to the story of the resurrection, I could see your eyes brighten, your countenance lift, and your hope grow. And then, finally, when you learned that Jesus had risen from the dead, a look of delight spread over your face, and you began to laugh with unspeakable joy.

As a father, I got to see you experience the story of Jesus's resurrection for the very first time. It was wonderful just to watch your childlike faith. There were no questions, doubts, or skepticism. You didn't ask for mathematical proof. You just believed. And you did so with great earnestness.

But it's hard to keep this same childlike faith when we get older. Now that you're in college, you're beginning to ask more questions about what you believe (and why you believe it). While believing in something like the resurrection felt natural as a child, it may seem more unnatural as an adult—especially in the university setting. You may begin to wonder whether it makes sense to believe something so crazy. Do we really think a person died and came back to life three days later? After all, we don't see that happening now, right? So why should we believe it happened then?

For that matter, you might also wonder about all the other miracles in the Bible. Do we really believe that the sea was parted for Moses? Or that the sun stopped in the sky for Joshua? Or that the wind and the waves stopped for Jesus? The stories may have seemed plausible as a child, but now they may just seem silly—kind of like believing in Santa Claus or the tooth fairy. Now we know better, right?

No, we don't. For one, Jesus calls us to keep our childlike faith: "Whoever does not receive the kingdom of God like a child shall not enter it" (Luke 18:17). On top of this, the argument against miracles is not nearly as compelling as it first seems. I want to use this letter to explain why we have very good intellectual reasons to believe in the resurrection of Jesus. And if Jesus rose from the dead—arguably the world's greatest miracle—then we have every reason to think the other miracles in Scripture could have happened too.

Are Miracles Impossible?

Needless to say, the most fundamental reason that people don't believe the miracles in the Bible is because they already believe something else, namely, that *miracles are impossible*. In other words, they have a worldview that rules out the supernatural from the outset. Thus, it doesn't really matter how good the evidence for a particular miracle might be. It doesn't really matter how many eyewitnesses there are. Such factors are irrelevant. Any claim to the miraculous must be rejected in principle.

Of course, this approach just raises the obvious question whether there are good reasons to think miracles are impossible. After all, how does a person *know* that miracles can't happen?

The skeptic might say, "Because I've never seen a miracle." But that's not a very good argument. Not personally seeing something doesn't make it impossible. There are tribes in the remote Amazon that have never seen snow, even in pictures. Their personal experience is uniformly against the existence of snow. If told that snow exists—white, fluffy material falling from the sky—they might insist that it can't possibly be true. But they would be mistaken.

Moreover, there are mountains of both historical and modern-day testimonies from people who *have* seen miracles. In fact, biblical scholar Craig Keener actually cataloged hundreds of these modern testimonies in his massive two-volume work *Miracles: The Credibility of the New Testament Accounts.*[1] So again, one's personal experience is not definitive.

At this point the skeptic could say, "Well, all those people who think they saw miracles are mistaken. They're all wrong." But that is a monumental claim. How does one know that *all* these testimonies are wrong? Have they investigated each and every one? Of course not. Moreover, this claim comes across as remarkably dogmatic. Everyone else is wrong, thousands and thousands of people, except for the person who is skeptical of miracles? While Christians are often accused of claiming that they're right and everyone else is wrong, here's the skeptic doing precisely the same thing.

The only way the skeptic could know that *every* miraculous claim is false is if he already knows that miracles are impossible. But that is the very thing that is being disputed. To assume miracles are impossible at the outset is to argue in a circle, as C. S. Lewis points out:

> Unfortunately, we know the experience against them [miracles] to be uniform only if we know that all the reports of them are false. And we can know all the reports to be false only if we know already that miracles have never occurred. In fact, we are arguing in a circle.[2]

Are Miracles Improbable?

Feeling the weight of these considerations, some skeptics will reluctantly admit that we can't know that miracles are impossible. They will still insist, however, that miracles remain highly *improbable*. So improbable, in fact, that we should never prefer a miraculous explanation over a naturalistic one. Given how unlikely miracles are, it is always more likely that a miracle did *not* occur. Thus, it is argued, historians would have no reason to ever affirm that a miracle actually took place.

Emma, one of your own professors at UNC, Bart Ehrman, has made exactly this argument. Given the improbability of the resurrection, he insists that we must *always* choose another explanation: "Any other scenario [besides a miracle]—no matter how unlikely—is more likely than the one in which a great miracle occurred, since the miracle defies *all* probability (or else we wouldn't call it a miracle)."[3]

Now, this sort of argument sounds persuasive at first glance. But it runs into some serious problems. For one, the probability of any event cannot be determined only by considering the event itself. The probability of that event depends on the broader context that surrounds that event. For example, imagine I was headed to a track meet and wanted to know the probability of seeing someone break a four-minute mile. I might think the chances of that are quite remote. But there's no way to answer that question without considering the larger context. If the track meet was just for local high school teams, then yes, the odds would be very, very low. But what if the track meet was for the Olympic trials? Then the odds would not be low at all. Indeed, *given that context*, it is quite likely that I would see someone break a four-minute mile.

The same is true when we consider the probability of a miraculous event. If a person believed that God did *not* exist (or at least did not intervene in the world), then she would view the probability of the resurrection to be very, very low. And she would be right. In a godless universe, we would have to assume that Jesus of Nazareth died and rose from the dead *naturally*. The odds of that would be astronomically small, especially after three days.

But what if the broader context included the existence of the Christian God—a God who has intervened, and continues to intervene, in the world? Then a miracle would not be an unlikely occurrence at all. Indeed, Keener even goes as far as to say that in a theistic worldview, "miracles might even be expected."[4]

Here's the big point: the probability of a miraculous event is contingent on a person's overall worldview and the assumptions he makes about reality. And this puts the skeptic in a rather difficult place. In order to claim that a miracle is improbable, he would first have to show that the Christian God does not exist. And if he cannot do that (and he cannot), then he has no basis for claiming that miracles are improbable.

But there's a second (and even bigger) problem with a probability argument against miracles. Even if an event is highly improbable, sometimes it is still reasonable to believe that the event has occurred if there's *good evidence* for doing so.

As an example, think back to when you were little and I used to play cards with you and John and Kate. Imagine a scenario in which I dealt each of you a poker hand with five cards and, after a brief moment, Kate loudly proclaimed, "I have a royal flush!" Admittedly, you might be skeptical. After all, the odds of being dealt a royal flush (without drawing additional cards) is about 1 in 650,000. Indeed, it is so unlikely, that it would not be unreasonable for you to explore other possible explanations: I stacked the deck in her favor, she misread her cards, she's lying, she cheated.

But a little investigative work would quickly rule out these other options. You could take a look at the cards yourself (ruling out that she misread them or lied). And you could consider whether I and your sister were reliable witnesses—ruling out that we cheated. And this would lead you, in the end, to conclude that the event had indeed occurred, *even if it is extremely rare.*

Imagine how absurd it would be if you said, "Well, I still don't believe Kate got a royal flush. After all, we must always reject highly improbable explanations in favor of more probable explanations. So I conclude that Kate must have cheated." No! The mere improbability of an event is not enough, in and of itself, for us to reject its occurrence. We have to consider other factors, such as the empirical evidence, the reliability of eyewitnesses, and so on.

This reminds me of the scene in *The Lion, the Witch, and the Wardrobe* in which Lucy returns from her first magical trip through the wardrobe. After describing the wonderful land of Narnia—and how she met a faun named Tumnus—her siblings conclude that she is just making up stories. Lucy runs off in tears. Later, Peter and Susan discuss the situation with the professor, worried that something might be wrong with their little sister. They are shocked to discover that the professor might just believe her!

Susan's response represents the classic position that miracles are impossible: "But this couldn't be true—all this about the wood and the Faun. . . . We thought there might be something wrong with Lucy." Notice that Susan's skepticism about the miraculous leads her to assume a *naturalistic* explanation, namely, that Lucy is mentally ill.

But the professor pushes back by pointing out that there's other evidence to consider:

> Why don't they teach logic at these schools? There are only three possibilities. Either your sister is telling lies, or she is mad, or she is telling the truth. You know she doesn't tell lies and it is obvious that she is not mad. For the moment then and unless any further evidence turns up, we must assume she is telling the truth.[5]

What makes the difference with the professor is that he is not closed off to the possibility of the miraculous. Thus, he does not feel compelled to always pick a nonmiraculous explanation. With a credible eyewitness like Lucy (who's more credible than Edmund), he is quite willing to think that a miracle might just have occurred.

The World's Greatest Miracle

Let's take this discussion and apply it to what is arguably the world's greatest miracle, the resurrection of Jesus.

First, the *broader context* around the events related to Jesus should be considered. Obviously, this includes the existence of the Christian God—who is quite able to raise anyone from the dead. But it also includes information we have about the identity of Jesus and why God might be particularly interested in raising *him* from the dead. Was there anything unique about Jesus that might make us think a resurrection would be more likely in his case?

Absolutely. We already know that God was at work in the life of Jesus. He was known, by both friends and enemies alike, to be a great miracle worker. He was known to cast out demons, heal diseases, calm storms, and even raise people from the dead himself. If there were ever a person in whom we might expect God to do miraculous things, it would be Jesus of Nazareth.

Moreover, we know that Jesus claimed to be more than a mere man. He claimed to be the incarnate Son of God, commissioned by his heavenly Father to be the promised Messiah and Savior of the world. And we have numerous Old Testament prophecies fulfilled by Jesus that appear to back up these claims—born of a virgin, born in Bethlehem, born in the line (and city) of David, and so on. Most importantly, some of these Old Testament prophecies even predicted that God's Messiah would rise from the dead (e.g., Ps. 16:10; Acts 2:27).

On top of this, Jesus himself predicted his own future resurrection from the dead (Matt. 16:21). That is quite a risky claim if you think about it. To predict your own resurrection and then not rise again would ruin your credibility as a prophet. But if you did rise, it would vindicate everything you ever said and did. Apparently, even the Jewish authorities were concerned about these predictions, as they stationed guards around the tomb to prevent any attempts to steal the body and fake a resurrection (Matt. 27:62–66).

What does all this broader context show? It shows that perhaps Jesus's resurrection is not as unexpected as we have thought. Given all these considerations, it does not look so improbable after all.

But we should consider more than just the broader context. Second, we should also consider the particular *historical evidences* that point toward the resurrection. Paul provides such evidences in the earliest testimony we have to the resurrection:

> For I delivered to you as of first importance what I also received: that Christ died for our sins in accordance with the Scriptures, that he was buried, that he was raised on the third day in accordance with the Scriptures, and that he appeared to Cephas, then to the twelve. Then he appeared to more than five hundred brothers at one time. (1 Cor. 15:3–6)

What is noteworthy about this passage is that Paul is passing along *earlier tradition*—tradition that scholars date back even into the 30s of the first century, soon after Jesus's death. That is long before the four Gospels were even written! This means that there was evidence for the resurrection from the very start of the Christian movement. It was not just an idea that someone made up at a later time.

At the core of that evidence is the *empty tomb*—"he was buried, . . . he was raised"—and the *testimony of eyewitnesses*—"he appeared to Cephas, then to . . . more than five hundred brothers."

The combination of these two things formed a powerful case for the resurrection. Obviously, if the tomb of Jesus had contained his body, then any early Christian claims that Jesus had been raised would have been quickly squashed. And the experience of the eyewitnesses proved *why* the body was missing—not because someone stole the body but because Jesus had risen from the dead.

But there's more. Beyond the empty tomb and the resurrection appearances, there's also another piece of evidence that is often overlooked, namely, *the continued existence of the early Christian movement.* Put bluntly, why didn't the fledgling Christian movement just end after its Messiah was killed? After all, the disciples were utterly demoralized after the death of Jesus, hiding in the upper room. To them, it seemed like things were certainly over. What could have turned it around?

To be sure, our historical records are filled with other messianic movements that predate Jesus—groups that claimed to have found the true messiah. But all those movements ended in the same way: their would-be messiah was executed by the Roman government. And then the group disbanded, demoralized and defeated. At that point, they could only begin to search for a new messiah.

So why didn't that happen with Christianity? Its Messiah was also killed by the Romans. And yet, inexplicably, the Christian movement continued. Indeed, it not only continued but also grew and prospered. Such an unexpected historical development requires a historical explanation.

And there is a historical explanation: Christians became absolutely convinced that their Messiah was not dead but alive. Thus, one of the best pieces of evidence of the resurrection of Jesus is the existence of the church itself. If Jesus had remained in the tomb, there would be no such thing as Christianity.

Other Explanations?

The above case for the resurrection is built on three pieces of evidence: the empty tomb, the eyewitness testimony, and the ongoing existence of the Christian movement. Even if a person rejects the resurrection, she still has to explain (and explain better) these same three pieces of evidence. Over the years, various attempts have been made to do just that.

Some have argued that perhaps the disciples stole the body and made up the resurrection so that they might start their own religious movement. But this theory is riddled with holes. For one, the disciples were not in a state of mind to march on the tomb of Jesus, to fight off the guards, and to stir up trouble with the Roman government. On the contrary, they were hiding in fear, scared for their lives. They were not thinking about launching a new religious movement; they were thinking about survival!

Moreover, it is hard to imagine the motive for stealing the body of Jesus. Are we to believe that these disciples, who had just sat under some of the greatest moral teaching the world had ever seen, suddenly became charlatans and hucksters? Now they are willing to lie for fame and fortune? The problem is that proclaiming the resurrection of Jesus did not bring fame and fortune. Indeed, it was likely to get them executed. Sure, people often die for lies. But they don't die for something *they know is a lie*.

Other ingenious explanations have been suggested. Some have argued that maybe Jesus didn't really die on the cross but merely swooned and passed out. Since people in the ancient world were primitive, they might have (mistakenly) thought he died and placed him in the tomb while he was still alive. Later, it is argued, Jesus awakened in the cool of the tomb and then appeared to his disciples.

But this theory is also deeply flawed. For one, it assumes that the Romans were not very good at executing people, which is hard to believe, given the cruelty and efficiency of the Roman killing machine. Also, Jesus suffered horrific physical injuries that—even if he survived them—makes this theory untenable. Are we to believe that after the most severe of floggings (some people died from this alone), six hours of crucifixion (with serious blood loss and dehydration), and a spear in the side (which likely pierced his heart), Jesus could somehow unwrap himself from the burial clothes, push back the stone, fight off the Roman guards, and make a convincing appearance to his disciples? Some might find this harder to believe than the resurrection itself.

On top of this, we would have to believe that Jesus himself was willing to *pretend* he was risen from the dead, effectively lying to his disciples. Aside from whether a great moral teacher like Jesus would lie, wouldn't it be more likely that he would express his anger over the fact that the disciples abandoned him and buried him alive? In the end, the theory just falls apart.

Most popular, perhaps, is the idea that Jesus's disciples merely *hallucinated*—they believed they saw Jesus alive when in fact he was not. But this theory, too, has significant problems. For one, hallucinations are not *physical*—you can't touch them, examine them, and eat with them as the disciples did with Jesus. In addition, hallucinations (by definition) are not something that happens in groups. How could the same people experience the exact same hallucination over and over? Can that happen with five hundred people? But the ultimate reason the hallucination theory fails is quite simple: the body of Jesus would have still been in the tomb. As soon as the disciples, and the Romans, realized his body was still there, then all claims of resurrection would have vanished in a vapor.

These are some of the other explanations for the empty tomb and the resurrection appearances (and there are more). And for those committed to a naturalistic view of the world, these explanations are all they have. But these ideas are riddled with such deep problems that it highlights again that the resurrection of Jesus remains the best explanation of the evidence.

———

While we can't return to our childhood, when it seemed easy to believe, God has given us very good reasons to still believe even as adults—solid historical evidence that Jesus has indeed risen from the dead. But we will not receive that evidence if we are not open to the possibility of the miraculous—open to the idea that wardrobes might just have forests inside of them. My hope is that you remain like Lucy Pevensie, believing in the magic of Narnia. And believing that Aslan is always nearer to us than we think. Even, and perhaps especially, when we don't see him.

Love,

Dad

Everything I Believe Seems to Hinge on the Truth of the Bible— How Do We Know It's Really from God?

The best evidence of the Bible's being the word of God is to be found between its covers. It proves itself.

CHARLES HODGE

Dearest Emma,

By now you've had countless conversations with your non-Christian friends. No doubt you've talked about a variety of theological issues—salvation, sin, repentance, church, morality, and so on. And in a university setting, you've probably also talked a good deal about cultural-political issues—transgenderism, immigration, abortion, and so on. Such topics have surely generated intense (and hopefully good-natured) debate and disagreement, most of which likely happens between 1:00 a.m. and 2:00 a.m. That's what college is for!

But in the midst of these conversations, one thing has probably become very clear to you. Your view of all these issues is drawn directly from the Bible. Even if the Scriptures don't explicitly address a topic, they lay out the principles and categories by which you can address that topic. Thus, whether *you* are correct depends on whether the *Bible* is correct. Regardless of the particular issue being debated, everything always boils down to the same question: Can the Bible really be trusted?

Of course, critics of Christianity recognize our dependence on the Bible. It's precisely for that reason that most attacks are directed at its reliability and trustworthiness. If the Bible can be undermined, then the entire Christian worldview falls apart.

So, Emma, I want to devote the next few letters to this foundational issue of the Bible's truth. But I don't want to begin in the normal place. Usually, discussions about the Bible's truth begin (and end) with a loud beeping sound—the kind you hear when an enormous truck is backing up, ready to unload its cargo. A barrage of historical evidence is then dumped out, burying the reader in a pile of facts and data, all with the expectation that such evidences will resolve a person's doubts and questions.

While there is an essential place for such historical evidences (as we will see in later letters), they don't always have the intended effect. Indeed, sometimes they can have the opposite effect—they can overwhelm a person and make her wonder if she basically needs a PhD in ancient history to know that God has spoken. Are the intellectual heavyweights the only ones who *know* that the Bible is God's word? What about the farmer who faithfully sits in the third row every Sunday? Is he (and most everyone else) just in the dark about the truth of God's word until he masters all the historical data? Surely not.

So I want to begin by asking about whether God has provided another way, a more accessible way, for the truth of his word to be known. Can a "normal" person really know that God has spoken? Thankfully, the answer to that question is yes.

God Has Spoken Somewhere

Okay, let's be honest. Sometimes it sounds rather strange—maybe even crazy—to say that the Bible is God's word. Are we to believe that God has revealed himself in a *book*? Really? It all seems so, well, ordinary. Even human. Why would God do such a thing?

But here's where we again have to remember the role of world-views. What seems strange or unexpected in one worldview may not seem so in another worldview. Certainly for the non-Christian—especially an atheist or materialist—the idea of God revealing himself in a book might seem downright preposterous. Who could believe *that*? In the Christian worldview, however, it does not seem this way at all. In the Christian worldview, it actually makes a lot of sense why God might do something like this. Let me explain.

We should begin by observing what makes the Christian God distinctive. Despite the claim that all gods (and religions) are the same, the God of Christianity is notably different. He is what we might call a *personal absolute*.[1] To say that he is absolute means that he is transcendent and all-powerful. He is the Creator and Sustainer of all things, self-existent and self-sufficient, needing nothing. But he is also personal, meaning that he is not just an impersonal "force" or a "power" but a living being who can, and does, relate to his creation. He loves, he saves, he judges, he shows compassion, he blesses, he curses.

Curiously, the idea that God is *both* personal and absolute is quite rare among religious systems—rarer even than one might think. Many religions have personal gods who are not absolute (e.g., the Greek gods). And many have absolute gods that are not personal (e.g., pantheism). In fact, it is only God as he is perceived and portrayed by Judaism, Christianity, and Islam (all of which claim a connection to Abraham) that could reasonably be considered a personal absolute.

So why does it matter that God is a personal absolute? Well, first, it gives us a very good reason to think that *God would speak to his people.*[2] If God is a personal being, and he created humans as personal beings, then it is quite reasonable to think that God desired a relationship with humans. And if God wanted to relate to humans, then it would require some form of communication. God would need to *speak* to us in a language that we understand and comprehend.

Indeed, there is an echo of this phenomenon in human relationships. Humans are personal beings made in the image of God, and we primarily relate through language of some kind. In fact, it is language, the ability to speak, that makes humans different from all other creatures. As Noam Chomsky observes, "Human language appears to be a unique phenomenon, without significant analogue in the animal world."[3] Perhaps this is why the origin of language remains one of the most profound mysteries for evolutionary biologists.[4]

But even if we conclude that God wants to communicate, we might wonder if he is *capable* of doing so. Perhaps God is trying to reach us but just can't find a way. Like the Greek or Roman gods, maybe he's frustrated with his inability to connect to us. But here's where we remember that God is not only personal but *absolute.* The Christian God made the entire universe and thus is quite able to communicate if he desires to do so.

So what does all this mean? It means that the very makeup of the Christian God already inclines us to expect that he can, and would, communicate to his people. If *that* God exists, then it makes sense to think that we might just possess some sort of communication from him.

If so, then that shifts the nature of the discussion dramatically. The question is not so much about *whether* God has spoken but *how* he has spoken. Put simply, our understanding of God strongly inclines us to think he has spoken *somewhere*.

The Pen Is Mightier

Okay, if God were to speak, then *how* would he do it? Well, again, the answer to this question depends on a person's worldview. Most people in the modern West have a profoundly individualistic worldview, in which God's main purpose is to make them personally happy and fulfilled, with little or no regard for how he relates to the larger community of believers. On that approach, we might expect that God would just go to each person privately and insert divine revelation directly into their brains. Indeed, this is how most Western people think God *should* speak.

But in the Christian worldview, things look very different. The God of Christianity typically operates not individually but *corporately*. His primary purpose is to reveal himself not just to private persons (though he does so on occasion) but to his corporate people (Rom. 3:2). Thus, we would expect God to deliver his word in some medium that was *accessible to all his people*. And there's a reason for this: it avoids the problem of having competing revelations.[5] If God did not make his word publicly accessible, then there would be no way for one person to verify what God had said to another person. There would be no objective way to adjudicate disputes about what God had *really* said. Indeed, false prophets (and modern-day cult leaders) regularly appeal to private revelations that are available only to them.

Simply put, "God told *us*" is more reliable than "God told *me*."

It kind of works the same way in a family. Remember our "family meetings" when you were growing up? Those were important times when Mom and I would communicate key family principles and practices. I suppose we could have pulled you and your siblings aside individually and told you the same things. But it made more sense to do it as a group. Hearing our instructions together created *unity* and *accountability* that would not have been possible otherwise.

Once we realize that God is concerned about his corporate people, and not just individuals, another consideration comes into play. God also cares about his *future* people. He wants to relate to them too. Thus, whatever communication he gave to his people would need to be delivered in a medium that could endure over time and be available for later generations.

Needless to say, there's one medium of revelation that allows for both public accessibility and long-term preservation: *the written word*. It was a technology available in the ancient world that would accomplish both these goals. The pen (or, in this case, the quill) was indeed mightier than the sword.

This is not to deny that God's revelation was transmitted orally at certain times. Oral tradition played a role, especially in the earliest phases of the Christian movement. But it was a limited and temporary role. It wasn't long before the apostles realized that they would need to preserve their testimony for future generations, and thus they—like the Old Testament prophets before them—put pen to paper and wrote it down.

There's actually a parallel phenomenon in the Greco-Roman world. Ancient historians preferred to learn about historical events through the oral testimony of an eyewitness—what they called the "living voice." But this did not stop ancient historians from keeping written records. On the contrary, they wrote down the testimony of these eyewitnesses *precisely so they might be preserved permanently for future generations.*

What does all this mean? It means that it makes perfect sense—given what we know about the Christian God—to think that he would not only speak but that he would preserve his words in a public, permanent manner. In other words, we have good reason to expect that God would have left us *written records.*

So maybe the idea that God would speak to us in a book isn't so strange after all.

Hearing God's Voice

Of course, even if we believe that God has spoken in written form, that doesn't yet answer the question of which writings are his. How do we know which books are from God? Has God provided a mechanism by which we can know whether a writing is divinely authored?

Absolutely. And it's not all that different from the way you identify the writings of human authors. You take what you know about a human author—style, tendencies, personal characteristics—and look for those qualities in the text. We might say we are looking for the "marks" of that particular author. So it is with a divine author. God's own qualities should be evident in any book that ultimately comes from him.

What are these divine qualities? Generally speaking, they involve the Scripture's beauty, power, and unity. God's word is *beautiful*, meaning it reflects the excellencies and perfections of God himself (Ps. 19:7). It is also *powerful*, harnessing divine power to do things in the life of the believer, such as bring wisdom, joy, hope, and peace (Heb. 4:12). Above all this, the word is *unified* with itself, cohering together harmoniously as it tells the same story of redemption throughout (Titus 1:2). We should expect to find these qualities in a divine book because, after all, they are the qualities of God himself. God is beautiful, powerful, and unified.

To dive a little deeper, consider just this last quality, the Bible's *unity*. People forget what a remarkable book the Bible is. It was written by more than forty different authors, over the course of more than a thousand years, in various geographical locations, within vastly diverse cultural contexts, and even in different languages. And yet, remarkably, the authors not only agree on a wide variety of complex doctrinal issues—salvation, eternal life, the nature of God, the person of Christ, and so forth—but join together to tell the same overarching story of redemption in Jesus Christ from cover to cover. How can that sort of unity be explained naturalistically? Are we to believe that these authors just randomly came together to weave a single, harmonious tapestry? It's hard to get four people to agree on much of anything regarding religion, not to mention forty, many of whom never knew each other. No, this is the sort of quality we would expect from a book that had a *divine* author.

What does all this mean? It means that *we come to trust the Bible because we recognize a divine voice in it—the voice of our God.*

In the ancient world, the life of a shepherd provided a ready illustration of this phenomenon. At night, sometimes different flocks would come together to stay in the same sheep pen. Mostly this was done for safety and protection. How, then, would the flocks be separated the next morning? Simple: each shepherd would call out, and *the sheep would recognize the voice of their master and follow him.* Jesus used this as an illustration of the way things work spiritually: "My sheep hear my voice, and I know them, and they follow me" (John 10:27).

It is worth noting that this is how most people in the world have come to believe that the Bible is the word of God. It is not because they analyzed piles of historical evidences but simply because they *read* the Bible and recognized that God was speaking there. This was true even of the intellectual elites. When the second-century pagan philosopher Tatian converted to Christianity, this is how it happened. It wasn't years of historical investigations and sifting through the data but the encounter with Scripture itself that changed Tatian's mind:

> I was led to put faith in these [Scriptures] by the unpretending cast of the language, the inartificial character of the writers, the foreknowledge displayed of future events, the excellent quality of the precepts.[6]

Now, at this point the skeptic will be, well, skeptical. She will argue that all this seems very subjective. "Of course you Christians *claim* to find divine qualities in the Bible. What else would you expect? But I don't see it. When I read the Bible, I don't see beauty; instead, I find it offensive. I don't see harmony; I see chaos. For that matter, if these qualities are really there, then why doesn't everyone see them? If they're there, then why do so many people reject the Bible?"

But this objection misses the point entirely. The Christian claim is that these are *spiritual* qualities present in Scripture. And to rightly recognize spiritual qualities, one needs the help of the Holy Spirit. Remember, not just anyone recognizes the voice of the shepherd. Only *his sheep* rightly recognize his voice. As I mentioned in an earlier letter, the non-Christian is not able to see and understand spiritual realities owing to the effects of sin:

"The natural person does not accept the things of the Spirit of God" (1 Cor. 2:14).

This reminds me of one of our favorite shows we used to watch together when you were little: *American Idol*. That program showcased some amazing singing talent from all over the world. But what made the show a hit was not just that it featured great singers. It was a hit because it also featured terrible singers who thought they were great! Each season, the same scenario played out. During auditions, a few overly confident singers would come along who were just horribly off-key. And when all the judges told them they were off-key, they insisted they weren't. The judges were wrong, they would say. They just knew in their hearts that they were fantastic singers.

This is a picture of the way it works with hearing God's voice. Think of non-Christians as those who are *spiritually tone-deaf.* They think they have an ear for beautiful music, when in reality they do not. So they "listen" to the Bible, and it sounds off-key to them. And they assume the problem is with the Bible, when in reality the problem is with their hearing. They need their ears fixed (by the Spirit) so they can hear the music as it should be heard.

In sum, coming to believe that the Bible is the word of God is ultimately a *supernatural* affair. Now, that doesn't mean it's all subjective. No, these divine qualities are objectively present in Scripture whether a person sees them or not. It's just that one needs the help of the Spirit to see them properly.

But What If I'm Wrong?
At this point, you may begin to wonder whether we can be certain that we've rightly identified these books as from God. After all, what if we're just wrong? What if we think we recognize God's voice and are mistaken?

There are several ways that we can confirm we are on the right track. First, we can look to the long history of God's people and ask which books *they* have recognized as bearing the voice of their Lord. If God is really speaking in the sixty-six books of the Bible, we might expect that there would be at least some common recognition of this fact throughout the history of the church. If we think we recognize God's voice in certain books, and it turns out that we are the only ones in the history of the church who have done so, then that might (rightly) make us doubt our own spiritual hearing.

But here we are standing on solid ground. There is a deep, wide, and long unanimity among God's people over the books of the Bible. I will explore this topic in more detail in a later letter, including questions about so-called "disputed" books. But for now, we can simply observe that we are far from alone in believing that these sixty-six books are from God. In the first century, it is clear that there was a great deal of unanimity over the books of the Old Testament—so much so that when the earliest Christian writers (like the apostle Paul) cited books as Scripture, they always cited books that are included in our current Old Testament. Such remarkable unanimity doesn't fit with the claim that there was widespread disagreement over the Old Testament during this time. As for the New Testament writings, the church quickly coalesced around these same twenty-seven books that we have now—a unity that has lasted nearly two thousand years.

Of course, if we are looking at others before us who've affirmed that these books are from God, we cannot forget the most important person, Jesus Christ himself. If we want to know whether we are rightly hearing the voice of God in these books, the opinion of Jesus would matter very much. Even non-Christians should give Jesus's opinion its due weight given his incredible moral teaching and unprecedented impact on the history of the world. And which books did Jesus think contained the voice of God? Well, obviously there was not yet a New Testament in his day. But Jesus quoted extensively from the Old Testament writings and clearly regarded these books as divinely given by God (Matt. 5:18; John 10:35). Moreover, he viewed his own words as equally authoritative as Scripture, laying the foundation for the future New Testament (Luke 24:44; John 5:39).

But there's a second way that we can confirm we are on the right track. We can explore the *historical credentials* of these books, asking whether there is evidence for their trustworthiness and reliability. Now, simply because a book is historically reliable, that doesn't make it inspired. But we would expect an inspired book to be historically reliable. After all, a false book would not be consistent with God's character as a truth-telling God.

Again, we lack sufficient space here to dive into the historical reliability of all the books of the Bible. That is an enormous task! But as we will observe in a later letter, the Bible has excellent historical credentials. As just a solitary example, consider the story of Oxford scholar William Ramsay. Ramsay was the world's leading scholar on the book of Acts, largely because of his vast geographical and archaeological knowledge of Asia Minor. In his early years as a scholar, Ramsay regarded the book of Acts as a second-century production, chock-full of inaccuracies and historical problems.

But Ramsay studied Acts further, testing the book's details as he traveled through Asia Minor, tracing Paul's journeys. And his opinion began to change. He discovered, contrary to his expectations, that Luke's narrative proved remarkably accurate—over and over again. Indeed, his mind changed so decisively that he eventually became one of the most ardent defenders of Luke's historical reliability:

I set out to look for truth on the borderland where Greece and Asia meet, and found it here [in the book of Acts]. You may press the words of Luke in a degree beyond any other historian's, and they stand the keenest scrutiny and the hardest treatment.[7]

Of course, there's much more to be said about the historical reliability of the Bible. But for now we can at least acknowledge that, under the most severe criticism, it has stood the test of time.

———

Emma, there is nothing more foundational, nothing more central, to your health as a Christian than maintaining a deep and abiding trust in the truth of God's word. I know that it is not easy to believe that God has spoken, especially in a hostile world that is always criticizing the Bible. But you don't have to have every question answered before you can believe. And you don't have to know piles of historical data to believe. Just like you intuitively know my voice, that of your earthly father, so you can intuitively hear the divine voice in Scripture, the voice of your heavenly Father.

And don't forget, Jesus himself believed in the truth of Scripture. As he said, "For truly, I say to you, until heaven and earth pass away, not an iota, not a dot, will pass from the Law until all is accomplished" (Matt. 5:18).

Love,

Dad

11

My Professor Keeps Pointing Out Contradictions in the Gospels— Can I Still Trust Them?

Now, as a literary historian, I am perfectly convinced
that whatever else the Gospels are they are not legends.
I have read a great deal of legend and I am quite
clear that they are not the same sort of thing.
C. S. LEWIS, *GOD IN THE DOCK*

Dearest Emma,

If you were trapped on a desert island and could have only a single book of the Bible, which would it be? You have sixty-six books to choose from. Chances are you would pick one of the Gospels. Maybe John. Perhaps Matthew. And there's a reason for that. Our four Gospels are the only sources that contain detailed material about the life and teachings of Jesus of Nazareth—what he said and what he did. That's why they have been some of the most beloved books in the history of the world.

The irony, of course, is that these same four Gospels have also been some of the most criticized and scrutinized books in the history of the world. And, strangely, they are criticized for the same reason that they are loved, because they are the only sources that tell us anything meaningful about Jesus's earthly life. If you want to undermine Christianity, then you begin with undermining the Gospels. If you lose the Gospels, you lose Jesus. And if you lose Jesus, then there is no Christianity.

No doubt you've already begun to experience criticisms of the Gospels in your religion classes. Professors are eager to take a swipe at their authenticity whenever possible, arguing that they are filled with historical discrepancies, contradictions, and fabricated stories. And such attacks can be troubling. Without any answers ready at hand, the average college student is just left with doubts lingering in his mind. Over time, those doubts can begin to erode your confidence in the Gospel accounts and thereby erode your certainty about what you believe.

But like most debated issues, you're getting only half the story in class. There's a whole other side to the argument that often goes unmentioned. So in this short letter, I want to mention a few other facts about the Gospels to encourage you.

The Date of the Gospels

When you were younger, one of my favorite family trips was to Washington, DC. We spent several days touring the museums, landmarks, and buildings, soaking in the rich history of that amazing city. Most fascinating was the National Archives, where we could—through very thick glass—look at the founding documents of our country, including the Declaration of Independence. That writing was the clearest articulation of why the colonists went to war in the American Revolution, a foundational and tumultuous time in our nation's history.

But have you ever wondered how we *really* know what happened during this period? How do we really know the details about the signing of the Declaration of Independence or the start of the war? The only way, of course, is to lean on historical accounts. But which ones? Well, in the study of history, it goes without saying that scholars typically prefer historical accounts that were written as close as possible to the event they purport to record. Imagine, for example, that we relied on a historical account of the Revolutionary War that was written in 1926. Such an account *may* contain reliable history, but it would be written 150 years after the fact. Surely we would prefer an earlier account (all else being equal).

Thankfully, we have earlier accounts. For example, we even have the autobiography of James Madison, one of the most influential of the founding fathers, an eyewitness to many of the critical events of this time. His autobiography was officially published in the 1830s, putting us within fifty or sixty years of the key events. And much of Madison's autobiography depended on his earlier notes. Such a scenario would give us good reasons to trust what we are reading.

So what if we approached the history of the Gospels in a similar manner? If so, then we would prefer (again, all else being equal) historical accounts that were written as close to the life of Jesus as possible. Like the autobiography of James Madison, we would want something written at least within fifty or sixty years of the events themselves.

If we ask which gospels were written within that range, the answer is pretty simple. Only four. Matthew, Mark, Luke, and John. Mark is probably the earliest, possibly as early as the 50s of the first century—a mere twenty-some years after the life of Jesus. John is probably the latest, written sometime in the 80s or early 90s. And there are good reasons to think all four Gospels would have used earlier notes and written sources (similar to how Madison wrote his autobiography). Indeed, these four canonical Gospels are *the only gospel accounts we have that are even dated to the first century*. All other gospels outside our Bibles are dated to the second century or later.

Take the Gospel of Peter, for example. This is what we call an *apocryphal* gospel, an account of Jesus's life that never made it into our Bibles. Though some scholars have tried to date the Gospel of Peter (or parts of it) to the first century, the consensus of scholars is that it was likely written in the late second century. That would be about 150 years after the events of Jesus's life, roughly equivalent to a historical account of the Revolutionary War written in 1926.

Here's the big point: the four Gospels in our Bibles are the earliest gospels we have and the only ones that put us in solid striking distance of the events of Jesus's life. If we are to know anything reliable about Jesus, these are the best sources we have.

Before we move on, let me just mention one implication of the early date of the Gospels. If they were written between twenty and sixty years after the life of Jesus, that means they were written when *people who had witnessed these things were still alive*. In other words, they were written when someone could step forward and say, "That's not how it happened. I was there."

We might say, then, that there was at least some level of *accountability* surrounding the publication of these four Gospels. If the authors were fabricating their stories, it is difficult to imagine how they would have been so enthusiastically received (we will discuss the reception of the Gospels in a future letter). Of course, this is a problem that later gospels didn't have to worry about. The advantage of writing a gospel in the late second century is that there would have been no one alive who could contest or challenge its content.

The Authors of the Gospels

Ever go into a bookstore looking for a good biography on someone's life? If it's someone famous, you may have a lot of choices. Imagine, for example, that you were looking for a biography of Nelson Mandela. If you had a choice between an anonymous biography and a biography written by someone who was a close personal friend of Mandela's, which would you choose? As it happens, there is an "authorized" biography of Mandela written by Anthony Sampson, a longtime expert on the politics of South Africa and a friend of Mandela's since the 1950s. Mandela gave him a commission, so to speak, to tell his story. My hunch is that you would choose this biography. It gives you the best chance of getting reliable eyewitness information.

When it comes to the Gospels, we are facing a very similar situation. If you had your choice of gospels, would you not prefer ones written by one of Jesus's closest friends, eyewitnesses to all he said and did? Or, at a minimum, written by a companion of these eyewitnesses who could reliably tell their story? If so, then you would want a gospel that at least has a chance to have been written by one of Jesus's *apostles*.

In essence, the apostles were Jesus's closest friends—originally made up of the twelve disciples. Not only were they eyewitnesses to all that Jesus said and did, but they were directly commissioned by Jesus to speak for him. They were "chosen by God as witnesses . . . to testify that [Christ] is the one appointed by God to be the judge of the living and the dead" (Acts 10:41–42). Thus, the apostles were given real authority to tell Jesus's story after he was gone. They were his "authorized" biographers, so to speak.

So that leads to a critical question. Do we have any gospels that go back to the apostles? The answer, again, is only four: Matthew,

Mark, Luke, and John. Matthew and John, of course, were part of the original twelve. Historical sources indicate that Mark was a disciple of the apostle Peter and recorded his teaching.[1] And we know that Luke was essentially a direct student of the apostles (Luke 1:1–4) and a companion of Paul himself (Col. 4:14; 2 Tim. 4:11).

As noted above, since these are the only gospels that go back to the first century—the time when the apostles lived—they are the only gospels with a *chance* of being apostolic. No other gospels, certainly not the Gospel of Peter, could be regarded as apostolic because, by the late second century, the apostles had been dead for generations.

Of course, this raises the question of how sure we are about the authors of our Gospels. How do we know that they were written by the names attached to them? Well, there is not enough space in a short letter to give the full historical defense of the authorship of each Gospel. But there are two lines of evidence that support the traditional authors assigned to them.

First, we have the testimony of the *church fathers*. If you think about it, the earliest Christians would be in a better position than we are to know who authored these Gospels. Thus, their testimony ought to bear considerable weight. As a test case, let's just consider John's Gospel. The earliest available testimony, even in the second century, quite consistently points to John the son of Zebedee, one of the twelve, as the author. Irenaeus, the famed second-century bishop of Lyons, is quite clear in this regard. So is there any reason to think Irenaeus would have been able to know such a thing? Well, there's little doubt that Irenaeus's primary source for much of his knowledge was his own mentor, Polycarp, the bishop of Smyrna. And here's the amazing thing: Polycarp was mentored by the apostle John himself.

That means that Irenaeus's information about the authorship of John's Gospel is only one person removed from the apostle John himself. Is it possible that Irenaeus *still* got it wrong? Yes, it's possible. Lots of things are possible. But is it *probable*? Given the close link to Polycarp, it does not seem at all probable. Put another way, we should not reject Irenaeus's testimony unless we have a very good reason to do so (which we do not have). In fact, Irenaeus's testimony about the authorship of John is confirmed by several other second-century sources, including Clement of Alexandria and our earliest canonical list, the Muratorian Fragment.

And there's a second line of historical evidence that points to the traditional authors: the *titles of the Gospels*. We typically don't think much about the titles, but they offer a powerful testimony that should not be overlooked. In short, here's what we find in the historical evidence: All the earliest manuscripts of the Gospels, as far back as we can go, have the same titles as they do now, namely, Matthew, Mark, Luke, and John. Of course, some manuscripts are fragmentary, and we can't see the page (or pages) that would contain the title. But for all those manuscripts in which the title page is visible, *we don't have even a single example of one of the four Gospels circulating without a title or with a different title from the current ones.*

Don't miss how remarkable this evidence is. If the Gospels *did* circulate anonymously (with no title) or *did* have different names attached to them, then how in the world does every single Gospel manuscript suddenly agree about who the authors are—without exception? How does such incredible uniformity just pop into existence? As a matter of fact, it doesn't. The uniformity of the titles suggests that they were attached to these Gospels from a very early time. And that is great evidence that the titles are a reliable indicator of authorship.

Here's the big point: if these four Gospels were written by the names attached to them, then these Gospels are not only eyewitness accounts but "authorized" eyewitness accounts. And that gives us a very good reason to trust their content.

The Reliability of the Gospels

Okay, thus far we've seen that our four Gospels are not only the earliest we possess but also the only ones with a reasonable claim to go back to the apostles themselves. In short, they contain the testimony of first-century eyewitnesses.

In order to test this claim, we can ask another question: Do they *sound* like texts from first-century eyewitnesses? Put differently, do the authors show familiarity with the geography, culture, language, and practices of first-century Palestine as we would expect? If an author were actually from a particular place and were an eyewitness to the events there, then there should be evidence for that in the text itself.

It's not that different even in the modern day. Think back to when you were nine years old, Emma, and we lived in Cambridge, England, for six months while I was on a research sabbatical at the university. It was quite the adventure. A new culture, new surroundings, new food, and even a new language. You had to learn the way words were used differently. A trash can was a "rubbish bin," a faucet was a "spigot," the trunk of a car was the "boot," and an elevator was a "lift." And there were also differences in day-to-day practices. Cars drove on the left side of the road, you paid for things in pounds, and people drank more tea than coffee.

Now, imagine that a person *claimed* to have lived in England but was *unaware* of most (or even many) of these cultural and linguistic distinctives. You would probably doubt that she had actually lived there. So it is with the Gospel authors. If they show a lack of awareness of first-century Palestine, then it raises questions about their historical credibility. On the other hand, if they show impressive awareness of that time and place, then we have good reasons to trust them. After all, they would not have been able to discover such things just by doing a Google search!

Needless to say, there's not enough space in this letter for a full-scale analysis of each Gospel and its awareness of ancient geography and culture. But we can lean on others who have done the work. In his book *Can We Trust the Gospels?*, scholar Peter Williams examines the canonical Gospels in each of these areas.[2] In terms of geography and topography, the four Gospels exhibit an impressive awareness of first-century Palestine, mentioning obscure towns and locales, accurately describing travel routes, and even providing details about buildings and structures. Again, how would one know such information without actually being there? Curiously, very little geographical awareness is exhibited by later apocryphal gospels like the Gospel of Thomas or the Gospel of Philip.

As another example, the four Gospels demonstrate an impressive awareness of Jewish names inside Palestine. The most popular male names in Palestine were Simon, Joseph, Lazarus, Judah, John, and Joshua (Jesus).[3] Even at first glance, that presents a remarkable correlation with our Gospels. Now, one might think such a thing could be easy to guess. But studies have shown that Jewish populations outside Palestine (e.g., Egypt, Rome) have a very different matrix of Jewish names. Someone fabricating a story from outside Palestine would have been unable to just plug in Jewish names he happened to know.

Here's the point: our four canonical Gospels show impressive awareness of the culture and context of the first century—and that is precisely what we would expect if they were written by the people whose names are attached to them.

Apparent Contradictions in the Gospels

Despite all these good reasons to trust the historical reliability of the Gospels, skeptics still have another complaint against them: *they contradict themselves.* These four Gospels, it is argued, simply disagree with each other in a number of places, proving that they cannot be trusted as witnesses to what Jesus really said and did. In fact, you may even have a professor who spends considerable time in class attempting to prove how passages in the Gospels conflict with one another.

At first glance, some of these apparent contradictions might seem particularly problematic, maybe even troubling. You might wonder how in the world there could be a resolution to them. But you need to keep in mind a number of considerations.

First, differences do not equal contradictions. I have been amazed at how often someone takes a mere difference between the Gospels and insists that it must be a contradiction. But the two things are decidedly not the same. We must remember that any given historical account cannot say everything. Some details are included, while others are left out. And different accounts often leave out (or include) different details. Such variations are inevitable.

Take, for example, the story of Jesus walking on the water. Matthew, Mark, and Luke all record this memorable miracle, yet only Matthew mentions the additional fact that Peter also stepped out of the boat and joined Jesus on the water, albeit briefly (Matt. 14:28–32). Is there a contradiction here? Not at all. Mark and

Luke don't deny that Peter walked on the water; they just chose not to include this portion of the story. Differences do not equal contradictions.

Second, we must be careful not to apply modern standards of historical writing to ancient texts like the Gospels. In the ancient world, it was not unusual to summarize stories, to change the order of stories (usually for thematic purposes), and even to adopt the language or literary conventions of the audience (so that the story was more understandable). Take, for example, the story of the centurion coming to make a request of Jesus. In Matthew's account the centurion himself comes (Matt. 8:5–13), whereas in Luke's account it was the centurion's *representatives* who come (Luke 7:1–10). Is there a contradiction here? Not at all. In the ancient world, it was not unusual for people to equate one's representative with the person himself—so much so that the two were interchangeable. Matthew probably just simplified the story by speaking only of the centurion himself.

Third, we need to remember that the words of a person were not always quoted verbatim as they are in our day. In the ancient world it was common to paraphrase, condense, or summarize a person's teaching. This goes a long way toward explaining how the same saying or teaching of Jesus in one Gospel might be worded differently in another Gospel. On top of this, it is very possible that Jesus originally delivered his teachings in Aramaic, not Greek. Thus, the words of Jesus in our Gospels—which were originally written in Greek—may already be a *translation* of what he said. This, too, may explain some of the differences in the precise wording of Gospel passages. Different authors are likely to translate Jesus's words in different ways (all of which could still be faithful to what Jesus said).

Of course, even with these considerations in mind, you may still come across an apparent contradiction in the Gospels that just seems unresolvable. It may be so problematic that you may think there's no way it can be reconciled. But here again we must be careful. Not seeing a solution doesn't mean there cannot be one. A solution may possibly be out there, even if we can never foresee what it might be.

A modern example might help. Historians Barbara Allen and William Montell recount the story of the 1881 killing of Frank and Jack McDonald in Menominee, Michigan—known together as the "McDonald boys."[4] These two men were suspected of murdering another man in cold blood. In response, the townspeople formed a mob to execute vigilante justice on them. But the various accounts of the deaths of the McDonald boys seemed fundamentally contradictory. One account said that the two men were killed and hung from a railroad crossing, while another account had them killed and hung from a pine tree. It was hard to imagine a way to resolve the disparate accounts. Then some old photographs emerged showing the men hanging in *both* places. Apparently, their bodies had been put on display in one spot, then moved and strung up again in another spot. Incredibly, and unexpectedly, *both* accounts were right.

Though this is a modern example, it makes an important point. Even if we don't currently have a resolution to a problem in the Gospels, that does not prove a contradiction. Further study may reveal a solution we didn't anticipate. And even if it doesn't, we can just regard that particular issue as *unresolved*. And that's okay. We don't need to resolve every single last problem in order to trust the Gospels.

———

Emma, I hope you are reassured that we have great reasons to trust our Gospels. They are the earliest accounts of Jesus that we have, they are connected to the original eyewitness testimony of the apostles, and they show great awareness of the historical time and place in which they were written.

If so, then we can trust the message these Gospels contain. John lays out this message as clear as anyone: "These are written so that you may believe that Jesus is the Christ, the Son of God, and that by believing you may have life in his name" (John 20:31).

Love,

Dad

I'm Being Told That Ancient Scribes Changed the Words of the New Testament Thousands of Times—Is That True?

*The evidence for our New Testament writings is
ever so much greater than the evidence for many
writings of classical authors, the authenticity
of which no one dreams of questioning.*

F. F. BRUCE

Dearest Emma,

As I mentioned in my prior letter, we have great reasons to trust the historical reliability of our Gospels. And that's encouraging. But there is still another objection lurking out there. Some have argued that the reliability of the Gospels is irrelevant, because we don't actually *have* the Gospels. For that matter, we don't really have any book of the New Testament. All we have are *copies* of those books. In fact, we have only copies of copies of copies of copies (and so on), all of which are different from each other in thousands of ways.

I heard this argument for the first time as a freshman at UNC, sitting in Bart Ehrman's class on the New Testament. Needless to say, it was quite disturbing. If scribes had irreparably corrupted the books of the New Testament, then how could I trust what I was reading? How could I be sure that the words I was reading in my day were the words that were written back then? For a moment, it seemed like the New Testament was turning into sand and just running through my fingers.

And Ehrman wasn't finished. We're not talking about just a few differences in the copies of the New Testament. He estimated that there were between two hundred thousand and four hundred thousand differences—what are called textual variants.[1] That's more differences than there are words in the New Testament! At this point, things seemed rather hopeless. If there has been *that much* change, then we might as well just give up on the New Testament altogether.

But like most controversies, there's always another side to the story. And when you hear it, you will realize not only that the New Testament text is trustworthy but that it might just be the most well-established text in all the ancient world. If it cannot be trusted, then no ancient text anywhere can be trusted.

The Quantity of Manuscripts

We need to begin by realizing that book production in the past was different from what we experience in our modern age, ever since the development of the printing press. In the ancient world there were (obviously) no laptop computers, spell checkers, printing presses, or other modern conveniences to help produce books. If one wanted to write a book, then it was done by hand. And if one wanted to see that book "published" and distributed throughout a broad geographical region, then copies of that book had to be made (also by hand). Thus, the New Testament was transmitted the same way every other ancient book was transmitted—it was copied by scribes.

Thanks to archaeological excavations over the years, and even accidental discoveries, we have access to some of these handwritten copies. They are called *manuscripts*. The only way historians know anything about the transmission of an ancient book is by the manuscripts still in our possession. In particular, historians would want to know two things: the *quantity* of manuscripts and their *date*.

Let's start with the quantity of manuscripts. Generally speaking, the more copies we have of an ancient text, the better. Why? Well, primarily it is because that allows us to *compare* copies. The more copies we have, the more we can see if, and how much, the text might have been changed. It can help us see the *extent* of textual variation we are dealing with.

But there's another—and maybe even more foundational—reason that the quantity of manuscripts matters. It gives us a higher degree of confidence that the original text is preserved *somewhere* in those copies. Even if one particular copy has been changed by a scribe, the original text may still be preserved across multiple copies. Textual scholar Eldon Epp explains, "The point is that we have so many manuscripts of the [New Testament] . . . that surely the original reading in every case is somewhere present in our vast store of material."[2]

So how many New Testament manuscripts do we have? Currently, we possess around 5,500 Greek manuscripts. Some of these are just fragmentary pieces; others are complete New Testaments. But this number is truly remarkable when compared to other documents from this period. Consider, for example, the writings of the Roman historian Tacitus. His history, called the *Annals*, is preserved in just thirty-three total copies (though primarily in just two copies prior to the fifteenth century).[3] Again, Epp observes the unique situation of the New Testament: "We have, therefore, a genuine embarrassment of riches in the quantity of manuscripts we possess. . . . The writings of no Greek classical author are preserved on this scale."[4]

What does all this mean? For one, it means we have no reason to think that the New Testament text has been lost. On the contrary, the high number of manuscripts provide good reasons to think we have the original wording, plus some variations thrown in. It's kind of like having a puzzle with too many pieces. One might say we have too much material!

It also means that we can gain a very accurate sense of how serious these textual variations are and whether they hamper our ability to know what was originally written. More on this below.

The Date of Manuscripts

As noted above, the quantity of manuscripts is not the only thing that matters. Their *date* is also important. Generally speaking, historians want as small of a gap as possible between the time a document was written and our earliest copy of that document. And the reason for this is obvious. Imagine for a moment that our earliest copy of the New Testament was from, say, the tenth century, nearly nine hundred years after it was originally written. A lot can happen to a text in that amount of time. Many changes could have been made. Thus, it is typically better to get a manuscript that dates as closely as possible to the time when that document was originally composed.[5]

In fact, when we look at classical documents from the same time as our New Testament, a large gap of time between their initial publication and our earliest copy is not unusual. Consider again Tacitus's

Annals. Tacitus wrote that work around AD 100, and our earliest copy is from the ninth century. Such a large gap is fairly common.

But the New Testament is an exception to this general pattern. Although the vast majority of New Testament manuscripts are dated to the Middle Ages, we have numerous manuscripts that go back as early as the second or third century after Christ. Indeed, some scholars have argued that in the second century alone we may have as many as a dozen manuscripts, covering over 40 percent of the verses of the New Testament.[6] On top of this, we have a nearly complete copy of John's Gospel (P66) dated to ca. AD 200.

Here's the point: the date of our copies means we have access to the text of the New Testament at a remarkably early stage. Of course, someone might still wonder if the text could have been changed even *before* that. Sure, it's possible that the text was changed even in the first century. But any significant changes made during this time would still be preserved in later copies. Thus, it is extremely unlikely that the text could have been meaningfully changed in the first century and then left no trace of those changes in later manuscripts.

The Quality of Manuscripts

Okay, so we have a lot of manuscripts of the New Testament, some of which are dated quite early. That puts us in a great position to answer the next question: How good are these copies? How many variants are there, and do they present a problem?

Here we return to Ehrman's claim that there are two hundred thousand to four hundred thousand differences between all these copies. Is that true? You might be surprised to know that the answer is yes. There are certainly this many differences and maybe even more (depending on how one does the counting). But before you begin to panic, there's more to the story. Statistics are only meaningful when you consider the larger context. And here are a few things that put those numbers into perspective.

First, we must remember that it's not just the quantity of variations that matters but their quality. What *kind* of differences are these? Well, you should know, Emma, that the vast, vast majority of these differences are *insignificant*. That is, they do not meaningfully affect our ability to know what the author originally wrote. These are ordinary, run-of-the-mill scribal slips that were common in any document from antiquity. For example, most of the differences between our copies are simply spelling mistakes. Yes, people in the ancient world struggled to spell too! Other insignificant variations would include things like word-order changes (e.g., "Jesus Christ" for "Christ Jesus"), the use of the word "the" (the article with proper nouns in Greek does not affect the meaning), and the use of synonyms (e.g., "Simon" for "Peter").

Obviously, such changes don't affect the meaning of a document. In fact, when we see such minor mistakes in the modern day—perhaps reading a blog article or newspaper—we either don't notice them or just intuitively "fix" them in our minds. Take, for example, the common English error of mistaking *their* for *there*. If you came across such a mistake, you would either automatically correct it in your brain or quickly look at the context to see which option the author meant. But the one thing you wouldn't do is toss the document in the trash with a dramatic declaration that no one could possibly know what the original author meant!

Second, in the vast majority of the cases when manuscripts differ from one another, we can reliably determine which text was original. Remember our situation as described above: we essentially have too much information. We have the original text plus a number of textual variations—like a puzzle with too many pieces. So is there a way to figure out which pieces "fit" and which do not? Yes, there's a whole academic field—called *textual criticism*—committed to figuring out which words were composed by the original author and which words were due to later scribal activity. While textual criticism cannot resolve every single variant, it can resolve the vast majority of variants with a high degree of confidence.

By way of example, consider Mark 1:14, where we are told that Jesus came preaching "the gospel of God." A few later manuscripts render this text "the gospel *of the kingdom* of God." So which reading was original? Scholars widely agree that "the gospel of God" is original. One reason is because it is attested by some of our earliest and best manuscripts of Mark. Another reason is that the shorter reading can explain the rise of the longer reading. A scribe likely added the phrase "of the kingdom" because he was used to seeing the phrase "kingdom of God" elsewhere in the Gospels. He was just harmonizing the text with other passages he knew (a common occurrence).

Mark 1:14, then, is a classic example of how textual criticism is done. Yes, there's a textual difference in our copies. But we can quickly deduce which reading was likely the original.

Third, the high number of textual variations is due not to a badly copied text but to the fact that *we have so many manuscripts of the New Testament.* The more manuscripts you have, the more opportunities there are to learn about new scribal mistakes. Imagine if we had, say, only five copies of the New Testament. Then we would have very few textual variants! Once you understand this, you will realize that numbers like two hundred thousand or four hundred thousand variants are not, in themselves, relevant. If it weren't for the great abundance of New Testament manuscripts— which should be a positive, not a negative—we would never even be talking about the high number of variations.

In sum, dramatic declarations about high numbers of textual variations, when understood properly, do not affect the reliability of the New Testament text. The numbers-only approach simply doesn't work.

What about Bigger Changes?

Needless to say, there's more to Ehrman's criticisms. Even if most of the textual variations are insignificant, not all of them are. Ehrman is quick to point out that some variations are quite sizable, including what is known as the long ending of Mark (Mark 16:9–20) and the story of the woman caught in adultery (John 7:53–8:11). In our English Bibles, these stories are usually bracketed off with a phrase like "The earliest manuscripts do not include the following verses."

At first glance, it might seem that these passages certainly threaten the integrity of our New Testament text. Based on just their size alone—each variant is twelve verses long—we might doubt whether we can trust our Bibles. But there are a couple of reasons why they do not present the threat we might suppose.

First, these sorts of large textual variations are decidedly rare. Indeed, these are the only two insertions of this size that made their way into the New Testament textual tradition. So it's critical that we realize that this sort of thing is atypical.

But second, and more important, these insertions would threaten the integrity of the New Testament only if we were unaware that they were insertions. In other words, if we *know* that these passages were added by a later scribe, then we don't have to wonder whether they belong in our New Testament. Clearly they do not. Thus, we have no reason to doubt the text at these points—we know what it originally said.

And when we examine these two disputed passages, we have

good reasons to doubt their originality. In the case of the long ending of Mark, it is missing from our earliest copies of Mark (i.e., Codex Vaticanus, Codex Sinaiticus), and early patristic testimony (particularly that of Eusebius and Jerome) indicates that most early copies of Mark lacked the ending. Similarly, we don't find the story of Jesus and the adulterous woman in any of our early copies of John (i.e., P66, P75, Codex Vaticanus, Codex Sinaiticus), again suggesting it was a later addition.

Of course, it needs to be acknowledged that for the average English reader, it *feels* like a problem to say that these texts are not original. Given that these passages have been part of our English Bible tradition for generations—largely owing to the influence of the King James translation—it can seem like they are being unduly kicked to the curb. And such a response is understandable. But if we step outside our English Bible tradition for a moment and just ask what was originally in the Greek text of Mark and John, then we realize that these texts are not getting "kicked out" of the New Testament. Instead, we realize that they were likely never there to begin with.

What about Unresolved Textual Variants?

While the situation with these two longer variants may be rather clear-cut, that's not always the case when we are choosing between variants. There are a number of places where we have competing variants that seem to be equally viable—though, on the whole, this is relatively rare. A good example is the famous passage in Luke that relates how Jesus was in such agony in Gethsemane that his "sweat became like great drops of blood falling down to the ground" (Luke 22:44). A number of early manuscripts include these words, and other early manuscripts do not. Thus, scholars are split over the originality of this verse.

So does this present a problem for the integrity of the New Testament text? No, because whichever option is chosen, no substantive teaching or doctrine is put in jeopardy. The message of the New Testament is still very much intact. We know of other passages, for example, that inform us that Jesus was in great agony in the garden even if this is not one of them (Matt. 26:37–38; Mark 14:34). And we also know from other passages that Jesus was a real human being who could suffer, feeling pain and sorrow (Heb. 2:17–18).

Indeed, this demonstrates a key principle you should remember. Not only are such unresolved variants very rare, but *none of them determine a key doctrine or teaching of Scripture.* No foundational truth is hanging on a passage with an unresolved variant.

Of course, some think we need absolute, 100 percent assurance about every last textual variant to trust the New Testament. Indeed, one gets the impression that this is precisely Ehrman's complaint. He writes, "If [God] really wanted people to have his actual words, surely he would have miraculously preserved those words, just as he miraculously inspired them in the first place."[7] In other words, if God really inspired the New Testament, *there would be no scribal variations at all.*

The problem with this approach is that Ehrman is working with his own self-appointed definition of inspiration, which sets up an arbitrary standard that could never be met. Does inspiration really require that once the books of the Bible were written, God would miraculously guarantee that no one would ever write them down incorrectly? Are we to believe that inspiration demands that no adult, no child, no scribe, no scholar, not anyone, would *ever* write down a passage of Scripture in which a word was left out—for the entire course of human history? Or was God prohibited from giving revelation until Johannes Gutenberg and the printing press? (But there are errors in printed Bibles too.)

Here's where we come to the nub of the matter. If God gave his word through normal historical channels, then we don't need to be surprised to find some textual variations. That's true of every document in history. And we don't need assurance about every last textual variant to be certain about the message of the New Testament. We are not forced to choose—as Ehrman suggests—between knowing everything and knowing nothing. God, through his providence and through normal historical channels, has *sufficiently* preserved his word so that the glorious good news of the gospel is fully intact.

———

It can be overwhelming to hear wild claims that our New Testament documents are corrupt and unreliable. But I hope this letter has given you the other side of the story. Unlike most documents from the ancient world, we have tremendous resources at our disposal—thousands of manuscripts, some with an early date—that allow us to see whether the New Testament text has been faithfully preserved. And the good news is that it has been. By God's providence it has been transmitted with remarkable fidelity.

When all the dust settles in these debates about the New Testament text, the essential message of the New Testament remains the same. It has not changed. As Jesus promised, "Heaven and earth will pass away, but my words will not pass away" (Matt. 24:35).

Love,

Dad

My Professor Says That Books Were Left Out of Our Bibles— Can We Be Sure We Have the Right Ones?

The fundamental irony of Christianity! The Bible,
as we know it today, was collated by the pagan
Roman emperor Constantine the Great.

DAN BROWN, *THE DA VINCI CODE*

Dearest Emma,

When you were growing up, one of our favorite movies to watch was *National Treasure*. Nicholas Cage plays the character of Benjamin Gates, a historian of sorts, who is on a quest to find a massive treasure secretly hidden by some of the founding fathers of the United States during the American Revolution. It's a fun adventure with lots of twists and turns and lessons from history.

But I think what made the movie so popular is the idea that there's more to our history than we think. People are fascinated by the prospect that our culture's most cherished beliefs might just be mistaken. The notion that there was a cover-up—and that we are only now, for the first time, realizing the truth—is very attractive. Whether it's the idea that there's an invisible map on the back of the Declaration of Independence or that the CIA killed John F. Kennedy or that aliens really landed at Roswell (covered up by the military, of course), we all love conspiracy theories.

The same instinct (unfortunately) is sometimes applied to the history of the Bible. People are drawn to the thinking that maybe what we're reading is not the whole story. Maybe there's another story—a truer story—that's either been covered up, forgotten, or lost. And if we just did a little investigative work (*National Treasure*-style), then we could discover what really happened.

And this is where we come to the idea of lost books of the Bible. In recent generations, there's been a fascination, really an obsession, with the idea that books were left out of our Bibles. Our collection of scriptural books—what we call a *canon*—is incomplete or even mistaken, we are told. Certain books are in there that shouldn't be. And other books should be in there that aren't. Moreover, we can't really trust the canon we have because it is filled with just the preferred books of those in power. The makeup of our Bibles is merely the product of political maneuvering in the fourth century, led by the emperor Constantine.

This whole narrative (or at least some version of it) will be repeated over and over again during your time at UNC, whether by professors or your fellow students. And it can raise doubts in your mind. What if we have the wrong books? Why these books and no others? Is my Bible just the construct of those in power?

I want to use this letter, Emma, to reassure you that the collection of books in our Bibles can be trusted. As you will see, the canon of Scripture formed early and naturally, long before any political or even ecclesiastical power could have put it together. Moreover, many of these *apocryphal* books (writings left out of our Bibles) just lack the historical credentials of the canonical books. They are often late productions with no reasonable chance of coming from eyewitnesses.

The Sands of Egypt

As we jump into this issue of lost books, I want to begin with Muhammad Ali. No, not the boxer. I want to begin with Muhammad Ali the *shepherd*. In 1945, near the town of Nag Hammadi, Egypt, a shepherd named Muhammad Ali was digging in the ground for fertilizer when his shovel hit something hard. Almost like something out of a movie, he proceeded to uncover an earthenware jar. After wondering whether he should break it open—out of fear that an evil spirit (a "jinn") might be inside—he decided the risk was worth it. Upon breaking the jar, he discovered books, thirteen leather-bound codices, to be exact. No doubt, this was a grand disappointment for a poor shepherd wishing that he had found gold or treasure.

But Muhammad Ali *had* found treasure—just a different kind than he expected. Although he was unaware of it at the time, he had stumbled on what might be one of the greatest archaeological discoveries in the twentieth century. This Egyptian shepherd had discovered what would later become known as the "Gnostic Gospels," a collection of books that contained a very different version of Christianity (and a very different Jesus) from the one we read about in our New Testament.

Most noteworthy in this strange collection was a writing known as the Gospel of Thomas. This bizarre gospel is composed of just sayings of Jesus, with no stories of his birth, death, or resurrection. It is less about how Jesus saves us from our sins and more about self-knowledge and personal enlightenment. Jesus says things like "The kingdom is inside of you" and "Know yourselves; then you will become known."[1]

Needless to say, the Gospel of Thomas has become the darling of modern scholars. If one is looking for an alternative version of Jesus—a version that fits with modern cultural preferences—then this gospel would be an attractive option.

In light of such writings found at Nag Hammadi, a new narrative is being woven about the state of the canon in the earliest centuries of Christianity. We are now told that the earliest Christians were in serious disarray regarding which books to read. Some Christians read certain books, while other Christians read different ones. No one could agree on much of anything. Apocryphal writings were just as popular as canonical ones and just as widely read. It was basically a literary free-for-all until high-ranking church authorities in the fourth century suppressed these alternative writings and imposed their own canon on the masses.

While this narrative is widely repeated, and rhetorically effective, there's just one little problem with it. It isn't true.

Tracing the Origins of the Canon

When we look at the earliest evidence we have for the emergence of the New Testament canon, we find something rather remarkable. Christians did not seem particularly confused about which scriptural books to read. On the contrary, they settled on a "core" collection of scriptural books—approximately twenty-two out of twenty-seven—by the end of the second century and probably much sooner. Generally speaking, this core would have included the four Gospels, Acts, the thirteen epistles of Paul, Hebrews, 1 Peter, 1 John, and Revelation.[2]

What's amazing is that there was, in a broad sense, rather little disagreement or discussion around this core. There were no church councils, no votes, no formal debates. It seems that the church just naturally settled on about twenty-two books rather early. Of course, there were some "disputed" books—typically James, 2 Peter, 2–3 John, and Jude. But it is worth noting that the disputed books tended to be the smaller writings. And this should come as no surprise. Smaller writings tend to get used and cited less often. Thus, it is quite natural that it may take longer for them to be recognized (and used) in different parts of the empire. But even those disputes were generally resolved by the fourth century.

We see this core canon present in a number of key second-century sources. Irenaeus, the influential bishop of Lyons, affirmed approximately a twenty-two-book collection around AD 180. Most notable was his plain affirmation of our four Gospels: "It is not possible that the gospels can be either more or fewer than the number they are. For, since there are four zones of the world in which we live and four principal winds . . . [and] the cherubim, too, were four-faced."[3] Aside from what one thinks of his rationale, it is clear that the Gospel canon, at least in the mind of Irenaeus, had long been settled.

At about this same time, a similar core canon was affirmed by other second-century sources, including the Muratorian Fragment, the earliest canonical list, as well as Clement of Alexandria, one of the great intellectual heavyweights in the early church.

As impressive as that evidence is, we can go back even further. In the early second century, Papias, the bishop of Hierapolis, plainly receives Mark and Matthew as apostolic Gospels (Mark contained the teachings of the apostle Peter). Moreover, he seems to know of other New Testament writings such as 1 Peter, 1 John, Revelation, and maybe even some of Paul's epistles. Beyond this, it seems that Christians were using New Testament writings as Scripture even *before* the second century. The book of 2 Peter refers to Paul's letters as "Scripture" (2 Pet. 3:16), showing that a corpus of Paul's letters was already in circulation and regarded as on par with the Old Testament books. Similarly, 1 Timothy 5:18 cites a saying of Jesus as Scripture: "The laborer deserves his wages." The only known match for this saying is Luke 10:7.

What does all this mean? It means that Christians were not, generally speaking, in disarray over which books to read. The canon was not a literary free-for-all. Yes, the edges of the canon were a little fuzzy and would take time to solidify, but the larger core of the canon was already in place at a very early time. And this was long before any church councils or authoritative declarations. The canon, therefore, cannot be chalked up to politics or the influence of Constantine. The emergence of the canon was organic and natural—from the bottom up, not from the top down.

If so, then we need to do away with the idea that the earliest Christians were in the business of "picking" or "choosing" books for the canon. There's a sense in which that is true, I suppose. But there's little evidence that the earliest Christians themselves understood it this way. They weren't so much picking books as *recognizing* books. They didn't give authority to books but simply acknowledged the books that *already* had it.

To ask the earliest Christians why they chose these books would be like asking someone why he chose his parents.[4] It's kind of a nonsensical question. People don't choose their parents—they've just been there from the start! That's kind of the way it was with the core canon. The books weren't so much picked by Christians as handed down to them.

But there's another important implication of this "core" canon. It means that the earliest Christians had a standard by which to make their theological decisions. These core books shaped the earliest Christian doctrines—about Jesus, salvation, the church, Christian ethics, and so on. To put it another way, the *theological trajectory for Christianity was already in place*, regardless of what was decided about the so-called "disputed" books, such as 2 Peter or 3 John. And this theological foundation would have helped the earliest Christians fight against, and rule out, later heretical teachings like those we find in the Gnostic gospels.

How Popular Were the Apocryphal Writings?

Okay, so if there was a core collection of New Testament books, about twenty-two in number, by the end of the second century (and probably earlier), then how did the apocryphal writings fare? In particular, how popular were apocryphal gospels like the Gospel of Thomas?

Well, there are a number of ways that we can measure the popularity of these apocryphal texts. One way is by observing the number of manuscripts they left behind. The physical remains of texts can tell us which books Christians were busy reading, using, and, of course, copying. When we consider the remains of Christian writings from just the second and third centuries, we see a remarkable trend emerge: the remains of New Testament writings far outpace the so-called "apocryphal" writings.[5] Put simply, the apocryphal writings were not nearly as popular as supposed.

We currently possess over sixty manuscripts (in whole or in part) of New Testament writings from this time, including such books as Matthew, Luke, John, Acts, Romans, Hebrews, and Revelation. The most popular is John, with eighteen manuscripts. In contrast, we have a total of only seventeen manuscripts in the same period from "apocryphal" writings, such as the Gospel of Thomas, the Gospel of Peter, the Gospel of Mary, the Protevangelium of James, and more. The Gospel of Thomas has the most, with just three copies.

This means that the manuscripts of our canonical writings outnumber apocryphal writings at a rate of almost four to one. In fact, there are more manuscripts of John from this period than of all apocryphal books combined. Thus, we have no reason to think that these alternative texts were read or used to the same degree as our canonical ones.

Beyond the number of manuscripts, we can measure the popularity of books in another way. The frequency with which a book is *quoted* by the church fathers tells us a lot about how much it was read, valued, and leaned on for its understanding of Christian doctrine. As a test case, we return again to Clement of Alexandria. As noted above, Clement was an intellectual giant in the early church. He was well read, and he liked to cite a wide range of literature, both Christian and non-Christian. Indeed, he would even use apocryphal material from time to time, including books such as the Gospel of the Egyptians and the Gospel of the Hebrews.

But—and this is key—there was a vast disparity in the frequency with which Clement cited the canonical Gospels as opposed to the apocryphal gospels. Indeed, Clement references Matthew 757 times, Luke 402 times, John 331 times, and Mark 182 times. In contrast, he cites apocryphal gospels only 16 times.[6] Once again, it seems that these apocryphal writings were not nearly as popular as we are made to believe. When compared to the canonical writings, they are hardly a blip on the radar.

What does all this mean? It means that alternative books like the Gospel of Thomas were not really contenders for a spot in the canon at all. As we already observed, Christians in the second century had settled quickly on a core set of writings as the source for their teaching, preaching, and theology. These so-called "lost" writings may be fascinating and intriguing, but they were not nearly as popular nor as widely used as the books that made it into our New Testament.

What Made the Difference?

So far we've seen that the earliest Christians rallied around a core New Testament canon from an impressively early point, even rejecting apocryphal writings along the way. Such early and widespread unity over books demands an explanation. What allowed the Christians to recognize which books belonged and which did not? What made the difference?

Well, we should not forget what we discussed in a prior letter. Remember the words of Jesus, "My sheep hear my voice, and I know them, and they follow me" (John 10:27). The fact that Christians recognized, at a very early point, that these books had divine authority suggests that they were indeed hearing the voice of their Lord in them. They were sheep following their master's voice.

But I think we can say even more about how Christians recognized the authority of these New Testament books. Part of what made a person believe a book was from God was *whether the human author was in a position to speak for God*. After all, not just any person could represent God. Such people would need to be given a special authority to do so—a divinely appointed office that allowed them to be a mouthpiece for divine words.

In the early Christian movement, these authorized spokesmen were the *apostles*. Originally, there were twelve of them, along with others such as the apostle Paul. When Jesus sent out the apostles, he reminded them, "It is not you who speak, but the Spirit of your

Father speaking through you" (Matt. 10:20). Thus, the words of an apostle bore special authority—indeed, the very authority of Christ himself.

Of course, the apostles originally delivered their authoritative message orally—by preaching and teaching. But what would have happened if they wrote their message down? The answer is not difficult to discover. Such apostolic writings would have borne the same divine authority as the apostles' spoken words. Paul states plainly, "Stand firm and hold to the traditions that you were taught by us, either by our spoken word or *by our letter*" (2 Thess. 2:15).

Here's where we come to the main point. The books that the earliest Christians would have regarded as authoritative would have been the books they believed to come from apostles (or at least from their immediate companions). Apostolic books, then, were unique. Those books, and only those books, would have borne the authority of Christ. This provides the essential explanation for why we ended up with the twenty-seven books we did. Simply put, *these were the books that the earliest Christians regarded as apostolic.*

Now, there are some important implications we can draw from that reality. First, this means that the authority of these books was not something that was added later. Sometimes we have the impression that these books *attained* authority over time, usually because of a church council or vote in a later century. But if these books bore authority because of their apostolic authorship, then that authority would have been *inherent*. It would not have needed to wait for some later church declaration.

Second, this explains why some books did not make it into the canon. They were rejected simply because they were not apostolic. In the second century, we can see this principle at work with a writing called the Shepherd of Hermas. This book was very popular in the early Christian movement and widely read. The Muratorian Fragment, however, rejected the Shepherd for a very simple reason: it was written "after [the apostles'] time."[7] In other words, its late date showed that it was never an apostolic writing.

This principle is essential to understanding the development of the New Testament canon. No matter how popular a writing might be, it could never be a candidate for the New Testament canon if it were not directly linked to an apostle. This principle also explains why many apocryphal gospels were rejected. Writings like the Gospel of Thomas, despite their title, were late productions that could never be credibly linked to an apostle. Therefore, their authority was always in doubt.

Of course, our canonical Gospels are in a very different situation. As we already discussed in a prior letter, we have tremendous historical evidence that they date back to the time of the apostles and were connected directly to the apostles or their immediate companions. Thus, they were accepted into the canon for a very simple reason. They were regarded as *apostolic* Gospels.

What about the Old Testament Books?

As for the Old Testament canon, there are good reasons to think that there was an established corpus of books by the time of Jesus. The first-century Jewish historian Josephus offers a list of twenty-two Old Testament books accepted by the Jews, which appears to match our current thirty-nine-book collection (some books separated in our canon were combined in his list—for example, the Minor Prophets were viewed as one book called the Twelve). For Josephus, at least, the Old Testament canon seemed quite settled: "For although such long ages have now passed, no one has ventured either to add, or to remove, or to alter a syllable."[8]

The comments of Josephus find confirmation in another first-century Jewish source, namely, Philo of Alexandria. Philo hints at a threefold division to the Old Testament canon: "the laws and oracles delivered through the mouths of prophets, and psalms."[9] This threefold structure seems to match Jesus's own words about the Old Testament being composed of "the Law of Moses and the Prophets and the Psalms" (Luke 24:44). Other echoes of a threefold division to the Old Testament can be found in the Jewish work Ben Sirach (Ecclesiasticus) and a fragmentary text from Qumran known as 4QMMT.

One of the other ways to ascertain the state of the Old Testament canon in the first century is to consider the way New Testament writers use Old Testament books. Even though the Old Testament is cited frequently by New Testament writers, there is no indication of any dispute over the boundaries of the Old Testament canon. Indeed, there is not a single instance anywhere of a New Testament author citing a book as Scripture that is not in our current thirty-nine-book canon. And while Jesus himself had many disagreements with the Jewish leadership of his day, there appears to be no indication that there was any disagreement over which books were Scripture—a reality that is hard to explain if the Old Testament canon was still in flux.

The fact that there was an established Old Testament canon in the first century goes a long way toward helping us know what to do with books known as the Apocrypha. These books include 1 and 2 Maccabees, 1 Esdras, Judith, Tobit, the Wisdom of Solomon, Sirach (Ecclesiasticus), and Baruch, as well as some smaller works and even some additions to existing canonical books. Written approximately between the third century BC and the first century AD, all these books are preserved in Greek, though some may have been written originally in Hebrew or Aramaic. The Apocrypha was officially added to the Old Testament canon by the Roman Catholic Church at the Council of Trent in the sixteenth century.

So what do we make of these books? Although they were known and used among the Jews of the first century, there is little evidence to suggest that they were regarded as Scripture. Neither Josephus nor Philo—key sources for our understanding of the scope of the Old Testament canon—uses them as Scripture. Later rabbinic writers did not receive the Apocrypha but instead affirmed only the Hebrew Scriptures as part of the Jewish canon. And, most importantly, no New Testament author (most of whom were Jews) cites even a single book from the Apocrypha as Scripture. Indeed, this is the primary reason why we believe the Old Testament canon should be restricted to our current thirty-nine-book collection, namely, because *this appears to be the canon of Jesus and the apostles.*

———

I know it is sometimes hard to believe that we have the right books in our Bibles when people are constantly raising doubts in your mind. Our world loves a good conspiracy theory. For some, it is always more attractive to believe that books were merely picked by humans in some smoke-filled room than to believe that they were given by God.

But the historical evidence is on our side. The biblical canon is not the result of some church council or political maneuver. It developed naturally, organically, and early. And that points not to a human cause but to a divine cause. The canon, in the end, is the result of God speaking to his people: "God spoke to our fathers by the prophets, but in these last days he has spoken to us by his Son" (Heb. 1:1–2).

Love,

Dad

Some Parts of the Bible Seem Morally Troubling—How Can a Book Be from God If It Advocates Oppression or Genocide?

Do those people who hold up the Bible as an inspiration to moral rectitude have the slightest notion of what is actually written in it?

RICHARD DAWKINS

Dearest Emma,

The last few letters have had a very particular aim, namely, to deal with the variety of attacks leveled at the truth of the Bible. And so far, most of the attacks we've examined have been historical in nature, whether it be textual transmission, the origins of the canon, or the existence of apocryphal gospels.

But recently, a new type of challenge has gained momentum, particularly in your generation. In years gone by, this sort of challenge would have been quite rare, even unthinkable in certain quarters. Now it might just be the most common attack leveled against the Bible. It's the claim that the Bible should not be trusted because it is *immoral.*

Just let that sink in for a moment. The Bible and the God of the Bible, it is claimed, should be rejected because they are morally deficient. I am sure the irony of that sort of claim is not lost on you.

Now, this shift cannot be appreciated without realizing how different it was when I started college in the 1980s. At that time, the culture wars were also centered on issues related to morality. But—and here's the key difference—most of the moral arguments were coming from ostensibly "Christian" circles. Jerry Falwell and Pat Robertson led the "moral majority," critiquing the perceived hedonism of the 1980s. High-profile Christian leaders everywhere were trying to lead the nation back to "family values." A short time later, Vice President Dan Quayle famously critiqued the TV show *Murphy Brown* because it glorified single-parent homes.

Of course, not all Americans welcomed this moral message. Indeed, many were quite put off by it. So how did they push back? Not by claiming their own morals were superior but by insisting that moral arguments should not be allowed in the first place. "Don't push your morality on me" was the mantra. Falwell and Robertson were chided for their self-righteous posturing. They were told to just keep their morals to themselves.

My, how times have changed. While the "moral majority" of the 1980s is long since defunct, something rather bizarre has happened in the ensuing years. The banner of moral righteousness has been picked up again but this time by non-Christians. A deep "moral outrage" remains in our culture, but it is no longer directed toward abortion, infidelity, and sexual promiscuity. Now it is directed toward the treatment of immigrants, the lack of women's rights in the Middle East, and sexual harassment. Now, to be clear, Christians have something to say about all these issues too. But the point here is that non-Christians are now often leading the moral charge. Long gone is the "Don't push your morality on me" mantra.

This new moral "awakening" within the non-Christian world has now affected the way people view the Bible. In years past, it would have taken a lot of hubris to critique the Bible on moral grounds. Most non-Christians (at least in the US) would have just conceded the moral high ground to the "good book." Those days are pretty much over. Now the Bible is as much in the crosshairs of the morality police as anything else.

So what are the main moral complaints about the Bible? We will consider the three main ones, namely, that the Bible condones slavery, oppresses women, and advocates genocide. Let's take them one at a time.

Is the Bible Proslavery?

On June 17, 2015, white supremacist Dylann Roof walked into a prayer service at an African American church in Charleston, South Carolina, and shot nine people to death. This unspeakable tragedy raised (again) serious questions about race relations in the United States. It seems the ghosts of our country's past continue to haunt us—the trans-Atlantic slave trade, the Civil War, and the era of Jim Crow. With both a past and a present like this, it is understandable that our culture is on edge when it comes to racial issues.

Given this context, it may be no surprise that some folks view the Bible with a bit of suspicion. It seems, at least at first glance, to support the idea of slavery. After all, doesn't it say, "Slaves, obey your earthly masters" (Eph. 6:5 NIV)? How can that be? Does that mean that God approves of this awful institution? As it is with many things, first glances are not the whole story. In fact, you'll discover that such knee-jerk reactions are often due to an insufficient understanding of the ancient world of the Bible. Here are a few things to consider.

First, slavery in the first-century Roman world was notably different from the type of slavery that modern people have in mind. When people hear the word *slave* today, they can think only of plantations in the antebellum American South, where slaves were acquired sometimes through kidnapping, had no financial resources, and were often cruelly abused. But the chattel slavery of the nineteenth century should not be read back into texts written in the first century. As strange as it sounds, "slaves" in the time of Paul were not necessarily destitute but were often paid a wage. Some were even known to accrue considerable wealth. Commenting on the social structure of the early Christian world, scholar Dimitris Kyrtatas observes that some slaves "managed to amass large fortunes and considerable property."[1] Beyond this, some slaves were highly educated. In fact, many slaves could read and write—and would often serve as the household "scribe" for employers who were themselves illiterate.

Moreover, how and why people became slaves in the Roman world was very different. For one, it was not due to their skin color or ethnicity. Often people voluntarily became slaves as a means to achieve a minimal level of financial security, and this was usually for a limited duration of time. It is precisely for this reason that many English translations of the Bible don't use the word "slave" but prefer the word "bondservant." The latter term more accurately captures the situation in the time of the first century.

Of course, this doesn't mean that Paul is commending this first-century version of slavery. We should not forget that ancient slavery could still be cruel and oppressive. As a result, he encourages slaves to gain their freedom if they can (1 Cor. 7:21). At the same time, we can't expect Paul to sound like a nineteenth-century abolitionist, rallying people to join public protests or to write to their local congressman (or Roman official, as the case may be). Instead, he was just trying to give his readers advice about how to navigate the world in which they found themselves, even if that world was flawed and fallen.

Second, the New Testament affirms a radical level of equality between slaves and nonslaves in the body of Christ. While the ancient Roman world was quite stratified, with rich and poor often in separate social classes, the Christian ethic was radically different. Paul's vision for the body of Christ would have been shocking to the average listener: "There is neither Jew nor Greek, there is neither slave nor free, there is no male and female, for you are all one in Christ Jesus" (Gal. 3:28). Indeed, Paul lived this out in his own life. In the letter to Philemon, Paul speaks of a runaway slave he's come to know named Onesimus. Rather than viewing Onesimus as a piece of property, he calls Philemon to receive him "no longer as a slave, but better than a slave, as a dear brother" (Philem. 16 NIV). Indeed, Paul says something even more incredible: "Receive [Onesimus] as you would receive me" (Philem. 17). Simply put, Christianity demands that a slave be treated with the same dignity as an apostle.

Third, when it comes to modern chattel slavery, Christians led the way toward its abolition.[2] Now, this is not the time for a history lesson about the intersection between Christianity and modern slavery. And the ugly truth is that some Christians—or at least professing Christians—defended the practice. And that is a dark stain on the church, particularly in the United States. But we must not equate the actions of any individual Christian with Christianity itself. The teachings of Christianity, rightly understood, were the foundation for the defeat of the African slave trade. For example, the Bible explicitly condemns one of the most horrific aspects of modern slavery, namely, kidnapping people and forcing them into lifelong servitude (Ex. 21:16; 1 Tim. 1:10).

Thus, many of the bright lights of the abolitionist movement in England and America were believers. Puritans like Richard Baxter and Samuel Sewall spoke out vehemently against the slave trade, laying the foundation for later condemnations by John Newton and John Wesley. This gave momentum to the British abolitionist movement championed by the likes of William Wilberforce. And in the United States, we can think of names like John Woolman, Benjamin Rush, and Jacob Green.

Here's the big point: The Bible needs to be read carefully within its original cultural context, rather than to be read through the lens of modern categories and concerns. And when reading it contextually, one will see that the Bible is anything but proslavery.

Does the Bible Oppress Women?

Another complaint lurking out there in our culture is that the Bible is antiwoman. In a world that emphasizes women's rights and equality of the sexes, sometimes the Bible, at least at first glance, can seem downright patriarchal. After all, doesn't Paul call wives to "submit" to their husbands (Eph. 5:22)? Rather than taking us forward, the teachings of Scripture might seem to be taking us backward.

As with the issue of slavery, however, first glances can be deceptive. Once we dive deeper into the biblical narrative, we find a vision for men and women having equal dignity and worth— a vision that would have been radical and countercultural in the context of the ancient world.

So how did the ancient Roman world view women in Paul's day? Generally speaking, it was not an easy world for women. The fact that women were seen as less valuable than men is evident in a variety of ways. One was female infanticide. It was quite common for female babies to be left to die, creating a significant shortage in the female population of the Greco-Roman world—so much so that the females probably composed only about one-third of the population in pagan circles.[3] Another indicator is the way women were treated within marriage. It was common in the Greco-Roman world for men to enjoy a great deal of sexual freedom—with concubines, mistresses, and even prostitutes—whereas women were expected to remain sexually faithful to their husband.

In short, things were not at all equal between men and women.

Standing in radical contrast to the ancient world is the biblical vision for women. We see this from the very first chapters of the Bible. Before God addresses what makes men and women different (and we will get to that below), he first declares what makes them the same:

> So God created man in his own image,
>   in the image of God he created him;
>   male and female he created them. (Gen. 1:27)

There's a fundamental affirmation here of the equality of men and women. They are equal in value and worth and dignity, precisely because they are both made *in God's image*.

This biblical value concerning women also shines through in the New Testament writings. And it begins with Jesus himself. Transcending the cultural taboos of his own day, Jesus talked with women one-on-one (John 4:7), befriended women (John 11:5), traveled with women (Luke 8:1–3), and even taught women (Luke 10:39). We are also told that women served in the ministry of Jesus in a variety of ways, even supporting him financially out of their own means (Luke 8:3).

We also see the value of women affirmed in the ministry of Paul. In the closing chapter of the book of Romans, for example, Paul offers a long list of greetings, acknowledging those who've helped him in the ministry of the gospel. It is noteworthy that nearly half this list is composed of women. Indeed, the very first name is a female, Phoebe, who is a noted "patron" of Paul and many others (Rom. 16:1). He mentions also Prisca (Priscilla), who hosts a church in her house with her husband, Aquila (Rom. 16:3), along with other women who are "workers in the Lord" (Rom. 16:12).

Elsewhere, Paul also pushes back against the sexual freedom of the Greco-Roman world by insisting that sexual fidelity in marriage applies to *both* men and women (1 Cor. 6:12–20; 1 Thess. 4:1–7). In the modern day, it is difficult for us to appreciate how revolutionary this call would have been. Paul was doing the unthinkable, namely, suggesting that men and women should be held to the same standard of sexual fidelity precisely because they are equal in terms of their value and dignity.

This positive vision for women by both Jesus and the apostles goes a long way toward explaining why women were so attracted to Christianity in the earliest centuries of the church. Despite the modern impression that Christianity is a hostile place for women, Roman women apparently didn't agree. On the contrary, they flocked to the new faith in droves. Our best estimates indicate that women made up nearly two-thirds of early Christian communities—basically the *opposite* of that found in the broader Greco-Roman world.[4] Apparently, women found the church to be a place where they could find honor, dignity, fair treatment, and healthy marriages.

Indeed, so popular was early Christianity among women that it was often ridiculed by Roman critics as a religion for women. Minucius Felix, for instance, records the criticism that Christians were recruiting from "the dregs of the populace and credulous women with the instability natural to their sex."[5] Let that sink in for a moment. In the ancient world, Christianity was mocked not for being antiwoman but for being too prowoman! That is a far cry from what one hears in cultural conversations today.

Of course, there's still the question of wives "submitting" to their husbands. Isn't that a form of oppression? Not at all. Here are a couple of things to keep in mind. First, a difference in role does not equate to a difference in value or worth. One can have a different role/function in the marriage without one member of the marriage being inherently superior to the other. If we regard "submission" as an entirely negative quality, then we would do well to remember that even Christ submitted himself to the Father in his earthly ministry (John 4:34; 8:28; Heb. 10:7). Yet this submission did not diminish Christ's own value and worth. On the contrary, it reminds us that submission is a Christlike quality.

Second, Paul's vision for submission leaves no room for any notion of a domineering, patriarchal husband. On the contrary, when we read further in Paul, we see that he clearly calls for a marriage in which husbands display love and self-sacrifice: "Husbands, love your wives, as Christ loved the church and gave himself up for her" (Eph. 5:25). In other words, Christian husbands are called to value their wives more than their *own lives*, even willing to die for them as Christ died for the church. I imagine most women would want a husband like that. Certainly that was true for the women in the ancient Roman world who joined the Christian movement in significant numbers.

Note also that Paul draws a comparison between the way husbands relate to their wives and the way Christ relates to the church. This is incredibly significant because it reveals the ultimate reason why God has structured marriage this way, namely, because *marriage is a reflection of the intimacy between Christ and the church*. And the roles in the Christ-church relationship are not reversible. Christ is the head, and the church is called to follow. The two cannot be switched. Thus, inasmuch as the structure of human marriage is a living metaphor of this divine marriage, we can see that it is not oppressive but liberating. It is a picture of the gospel.

Obviously, there's much more that could be said about gender and the Bible than we are able to address here. But as for the charge that the Bible promotes the oppression of women, nothing could be further from the truth.

Of course, some will insist that they still don't like the Bible's vision for men and women. Fair enough. But we have to remember that not liking something is not an argument. Not liking something doesn't make it untrue. In fact, such dislike might just have more to do with one's own cultural preferences than it does with what is morally right or wrong. As already noted, we have to be very careful that we don't take our modern, twenty-first-century sensibilities and impose them on the Bible.

Does God Commit Genocide?

Armenia. Cambodia. Rwanda. Bosnia. Darfur. All well-known modern examples of genocide where entire people groups have been wiped out (or nearly so). These are awful tragedies, worthy of our sorrow and grief. And yet, ask the critics, is the God of the

Bible really any different? When the Israelites entered the land of Canaan, was it not God who commanded them to wipe out all the indigenous people (Deut. 20:17)? Is God not guilty of genocide? It makes me think of the infamous bumper-sticker quote "The only difference between God and Adolf Hitler is that God is more proficient at genocide."

Admittedly, this is a difficult, complex issue. We feel obligated, understandably, to find a way to get God "off the hook" for the deaths of so many people. Many possibilities come to mind for how that might be done. Maybe we've misread the passage. Maybe it's just symbolic. Maybe the Israelites misunderstood God's command. And so on. But in the end, I don't think we need to get God off the hook. I don't think he wants off the hook. As painful as this issue is, it highlights what we, and our culture, need to hear more than ever: God is holy, people are sinful, the world is broken, and his judgment is just.

If we are going to rightly understand the destruction of the Canaanites, several principles must be remembered. First, *every human being on the planet deserves God's judgment, not just the Canaanites.* Right now, all humans everywhere—from the kind old lady who lives next door to the hardened criminal on death row—are deeply sinful. And they were born this way. Since birth, all human beings stand guilty, not only for their own sins but for the sin of Adam, which has been passed down to them (Rom. 5:12). And the penalty for our sin is clear: "The wages of sin is death" (Rom. 6:23).

So what does this mean? This means that, at any moment, God could take the life of any human as judgment for his or her sins. And he would be totally justified in doing so. God owes salvation to no one. And this quickly changes our perspective on the Canaanite conquest. Rather than being surprised that God would finally judge people for their sins (even in great numbers), perhaps we should be shocked that he waits so long to do it. Every one of us is alive and breathing solely by God's incredible patience and grace.

Second, *the timing of God's judgment doesn't always match human expectations*. Sometimes we think God should judge the most sinful people first and work down the list. But, of course, God doesn't always work the way we expect. In fact, Jesus made this exact point when he was asked why the tower of Siloam fell and killed eighteen people. Jesus replied, "Do you think that they were worse offenders than all the others who lived in Jerusalem? No, I tell you; but unless you repent, you will all likewise perish" (Luke 13:4–5). Ouch. In other words, people don't have to be the worst of sinners to receive God's judgment. God is not obligated to judge all people simultaneously.

While the Canaanites were not the only sinful people in the world, and not necessarily even the worst, their sins were quite egregious. God drove them out of the land primarily because their practices were "abominable" in his sight—gross idolatry, use of sorcerers and mediums, sexual perversions, and even sacrificing their own children to the gods (Deut. 18:9–14). Despite these practices, God had been incredibly patient with the inhabitants of Canaan for generation after generation, dating back even to the time of Abraham (Gen. 15:13–16). But God's patience had run out.

Third, *God uses a variety of instruments to accomplish his judgment*. Sure, God could just miraculously take all the lives of the Canaanites in a single instance. But he has a history of using various means to bring judgment. Throughout Scripture, such means have included natural disasters, disease and pestilence, drought, economic collapse, and, yes, even *human armies*. At numerous points throughout biblical history, God "raises up" a human army to accomplish his purposes. And in the Canaanite conquest, God used the nation of Israel as his instrument of judgment.

It is here that we come to a key difference between the Canaanite conquest and modern-day genocide. Yes, both involve great loss of life. And both involve human armies. But the former is done as an instrument of God's righteous judgment, whereas the latter is humans murdering others for their own purposes. On the surface, there may be similarities. But they are decidedly not the same act.

An example might help. Imagine a scenario in which one human injects another human with a deadly toxin, causing that person to die. Is that murder? Well, it depends. If this were done by a criminal who wanted to knock off a rival, then the answer would be yes. But if this were done by an official at a federal prison who was authorized by the state to administer lethal injection, then the answer would be no. On the surface, the two acts might look the same. But everything comes down to whether the *taking of life is properly authorized*. The issue is not whether a life is taken but how and why it is taken.

Let me try to draw all this together. If every human deserves judgment (and we do), and if God is justified in taking a life whenever he decides to execute that judgment (and he is), and if God uses various instruments for that judgment (including human armies), then there is nothing immoral about the Canaanite conquest. Indeed, to object to the conquest would require us to object to *all* God's acts of judgment. Do we also object to Noah's flood or to the destruction of Sodom and Gomorrah or to the plagues on Egypt?

In the end, then, the objection against the Canaanite conquest is really just a general objection against God judging anyone at all.

And if we take that away, then we are left with something other than the God of Christianity.

"Don't Push Your Morals on Me"?

We've spent this letter dealing with three particular moral objections to the Bible, namely, that it is proslavery, that it is antiwoman, and that it encourages genocide. As we've seen, none of these objections actually holds up.

But for those who make these objections, the tables can be turned. Indeed, there is a problem that the *skeptic* has to deal with. If the Bible is morally problematic, then it must be violating some moral norm in the universe. It must fail to live up to the way things *ought* to be. So the skeptic then must answer the question about where these moral norms come from. By what standard are they declaring that the women *ought* to be treated a certain way or that slavery *ought* to be eliminated?

Of course, here's where we return to the theme of moral absolutes. I argued in prior letters that the only cogent foundation for morality is God himself. And not just any God but a God who is a *personal absolute*. In other words, the God of the Bible.

Needless to say, the irony here is thick. Skeptics are appealing to a moral standard in order to object to the God of the Bible. But they need the God of the Bible in order to have a coherent moral standard in the first place. In effect, they are sawing off the branch they are sitting on.

So it looks like the age of "Don't push your morals on me" is decidedly over. Modern skeptics are quite willing to make absolute, even dogmatic, moral claims about the Bible, about Christianity, and about a great many things. Unfortunately, however, they have no foundation in their worldview to account for these morals.

Indeed, if their worldview were true, there would be no moral norms in the first place.

This means that the people who have the real moral problem with slavery, the mistreatment of women, and genocide are not the Christians but the non-Christians. They may not like these things, but without Christianity, they have no basis to object to them.

———

Issues about the Bible's moral goodness can be difficult and complex. Topics related to slavery, gender, and genocide need to be explored carefully and patiently. But as we've seen, these objections tend to evaporate upon closer scrutiny. We need to resist judging the Bible on the basis of modern cultural preferences and instead need to evaluate it on its own terms and in its own world. And when we do that, we see that it affirms the worth, equality, and dignity of all human beings.

Love,

Dad

15

Sometimes It Feels Like My Faith Is Slipping Away—How Do I Handle Doubts about What I Believe?

*But there is a sort of attack on the emotions which
can still be tried. It turns on making him feel
. . . that all his religion has been a fantasy.*
C. S. LEWIS, *THE SCREWTAPE LETTERS*

Dearest Emma,

By now, you've read the many letters I have written to you. Together, they've all had a singular purpose, namely, to encourage you in your faith and to remind you of the truth of what you believe. And I hope they've accomplished that, at least to some extent.

But here's a reality you need to face. Even with many good reasons to believe, every believer still struggles with doubt. There will be times—and maybe you've already experienced them—when you wonder whether everything you believe is a lie. Maybe *we* are the ones who are deceived, you might think. Maybe all the critics

217

are actually right. Maybe this whole "Jesus thing" is just a religious experience, no different (and no better) than the experiences of the Buddhists, Hindus, or Muslims.

Put simply, maybe we're just *wrong*.

Now, these sorts of doubts can be very weighty. And sometimes they can be very painful to work through. It can feel like your whole life, your whole identity, even your whole future, hangs in the balance.

While such doubts are tough enough to handle in and of themselves, they are exacerbated by our current cultural climate. Many voices today—even so-called "Christian" voices—insist that the problem with evangelicals is that they are far too certain about what they believe. Indeed, certainty is now viewed as the supreme vice. And doubt is presented as the ultimate virtue. The epitome of intellectual sophistication, we are told, is to question everything you believe (which, of course, backfires because you would also have to question your questioning!). This group will cheer on your doubts, encouraging you to leave behind any confidence you have about the truth of Christianity.

On the flip side, other segments of Christianity heap scorn on anyone who doubts. They tell you that good Christians never struggle with what they believe. You just have to accept everything you're told, no questions asked. In such circles, there's no room for dealing with people's intellectual objections or concerns. Simplistically, we are told to "just believe." It can feel very suffocating.

With these two competing perspectives out there, it is easy to feel caught in the middle. But thankfully, these are not our only two options. In this letter, I hope to lay out a better path forward—a path that can help provide some balance and comfort as you work through periods of doubt.

No, There's Nothing Wrong with You

Okay, the first thing to get on the table is that doubts don't make you a bad Christian. I know that sometimes it can feel that they do. Whenever we question our beliefs, we can begin to think we have failed in some way. Perhaps we are just a second-tier believer. We feel like we've let God down, as well as our family and friends. We might even look to the great heroes of the faith and marvel at how they always seemed so sure and steady in their faith. If only we could be more like them, we think.

But here's the reality. Even the heroes of our faith struggled with doubt. Indeed, every believer, at some level, has labored through questions about what they believe. Consider the great Reformer Martin Luther. It's easy to marvel at his strength, fortitude, and courage in the face of unspeakable opposition. But you may not know that he struggled intensely with serious doubt and despair, what we might call "the dark night of the soul." Luther doubted his own faith, questioned his calling, and even wondered whether God had turned his back on him. So intense were his doubts that he labored through tears, anxiety, terrors, and bouts of deep depression. His friend Philipp Melanchthon even feared that Luther was on the verge of death.

The great nineteenth-century Baptist preacher C. H. Spurgeon was the same. Though it would be easy to be impressed by his preaching skills, enormous church, and extensive ministry, Spurgeon had his own seasons of doubt. At one point he confessed his struggle: "On a sudden, the thought crossed my mind—which I abhorred but could not conquer—that there was no God, no Christ, no Heaven, no hell, that all my prayers were but a farce, and that I might as well have whistled to the winds or spoken to the howling waves."[1] In fact, Spurgeon struggled with deep depression and anxiety for much of his life over such matters.

Here's the point, Emma: It's normal to struggle with doubt in the Christian life. It doesn't mean something is wrong with you. The issue is not whether you face doubt but how you respond to it.

Different Kinds of Doubt

So what do we mean exactly by the word *doubt*? As for a definition, we can begin with what doubt is *not*. Doubt is not the same as *unbelief*. Unfortunately, many Christians equate the two, which is why they feel so guilty about their doubts. They assume it means that they are rebels—people who just stubbornly refuse to believe God. But this misconception needs to be done away with once and for all. Doubt is not the same as being an unbeliever.

What then is doubt? Os Guinness offers a helpful definition: "Doubt is a state of mind in suspension between faith and unbelief so that it is neither of them wholly and it is each only partly."[2] In other words, doubt is a form of wavering; it's to be of "two minds" about something.

While doubt is not the same as unbelief, it may lead to unbelief if left unchecked. Thus, the Scriptures consistently call us away from doubt and toward our faith. When Jesus describes the way we should pray, he says, "Have faith and do not doubt" (Matt. 21:21). And James tells us that doubting can lead to an unstable life: "Let him ask in faith, with no doubting, for the one who doubts is like a wave of the sea that is driven and tossed by the wind" (James 1:6).

In short, doubt can be a hindrance to our faith. Indeed, it can be quite serious. But it is not the same thing as a lack of faith. And God is very patient with those who struggle with doubts. Jesus himself was very long-suffering with the doubts of the disciples, even showing great patience with Thomas, who insisted that he would not believe until he put his hands in Jesus's side (John 20:27).

Okay, with that definition in hand, let's now look at two different species of doubt. The first, and perhaps the main kind, of doubt that people experience is doubt about the *truth of Christianity*. Such doubts might involve questioning core Christian beliefs such as the reliability of the Bible, the reality of the resurrection, the divinity of Jesus, or maybe even the existence of God. These sorts of doubts are more *intellectual* in nature, though (as we shall see below) they can be caused by a variety of factors, some of which are circumstantial and even emotional.

The good news about this sort of doubt is that there are more straightforward, concrete ways to address it. If a person has a genuine intellectual question, we have great resources available to answer such questions. That doesn't mean people's doubts are automatically "cured" by simply reading a few books. But sometimes gaining a basic understanding of the facts goes a long way. Sometimes people have just never heard a solid answer to their questions. Unfortunately, as we will see below, other kinds of doubt are much more complex and difficult to treat.

Before moving on, one clarification is in order. As we try to overcome intellectual doubts and achieve a level of certainty about what we believe, that doesn't mean we must be *equally* certain about every belief we hold. There are core truths that demand more certainty than more peripheral ones. If you have doubts about the proper mode of baptism (immersion versus sprinkling), surely that is not the same thing as having doubts about whether Jesus rose from the dead. Questioning the former should occasion little anxiety, whereas questioning the latter can have serious consequence on one's Christian life (if left unchecked).

Now let's consider a second kind of doubt. Rather than questioning the truthfulness of Christianity, sometimes we use the word *doubt* just to describe how we are *struggling with some aspect of the Christian life.* This might involve feeling like you don't understand God, being confused by a particular doctrine, or wanting to know why God did (or did not do) something. This kind of doubt can also entail doubts about *ourselves*: Am I really a Christian? Does God really love me? Is he really going to provide for my needs?

This second kind of doubt is also prevalent in the Bible. Indeed, it could be understood more as a form of struggle, worry, anxiety, or even fear. Consider the apostle Paul and his anguish over the "thorn" in the flesh (2 Cor. 12:7). This was a painful crisis for Paul, causing him to plead three times for its removal, even wondering why God refused to do so. The psalmist often expresses a similar sort of struggle. Bad things happen, and God seems distant, far away, and uncaring. At one point, he feels abandoned by God:

> Awake! Why are you sleeping, O Lord?
> Rouse yourself! Do not reject us forever! (Ps. 44:23)

We should observe that this second kind of doubt is not necessarily sinful. It is often just part of life in a fallen world. It's not so much that we doubt the truthfulness of God's word (that's the first kind of doubt); it may just be that we are struggling to understand God and his ways. Or we might be doubting ourselves and the state of our own heart.

Regardless, we also need to fight against this second form of doubt. It, too, can wreak havoc in the Christian life if left unchecked, resulting in despair, discouragement, and even depression. Moreover, sometimes this second kind of doubt can actually lead to the first kind of doubt. The two are often intertwined and not easily separated.

Tracing the Source of Doubt

So why do Christians doubt? And what can explain why some Christians doubt more than others? The answers to those questions are lengthy and complex, but we can at least explore a few of the main reasons why people doubt, so that we can begin mapping out how to respond.

Unanswered Questions

Some people's doubts center on real unanswered intellectual questions about Christianity. They may have always had these questions but never received solid answers. Thus, they have labored through the Christian life with a faith that is weak and shaky. We've covered some of the main intellectual questions in the letters I have written to you: How do I explain the thousands of textual variants? What about apparent contradictions in the Gospels? How can Christianity be the only right religion? But a believer might also have practical questions: Why doesn't God answer my prayers? Why did my sister get cancer? How do I know if I am really saved?

Of course, you should keep in mind that just because a person *says* his doubts are primarily intellectual does not mean his doubts actually are. Sometimes the intellectual questions function as a "front" of sorts, masking the real cause of doubt that lies underneath. And that leads us to other reasons why people doubt.

Immoral Behavior

Believe it or not, one of the most common causes of people doubting their faith is that they are engaged in behavior that the Bible plainly forbids. This is particularly the case for believers who head off to college and get pulled into the wrong crowd. Soon they find themselves engaged in behaviors they know are wrong (sleeping with their boyfriend, getting drunk at parties, etc.). It's almost inevitable that such behavioral change is followed by a change in belief (or at least the beginnings of it). Those people will begin to say things like "I'm not sure I believe in God anymore" or "I'm not sure I really think the Bible is true." These objections sound intellectual, but in reality they can be traced back to their new lifestyle and their unwillingness to give it up.

A key principle can be seen here. It's not just belief that affects behavior, but it's also *behavior that affects belief*. When we don't obey God, we can begin to doubt God. Indeed, if we don't obey God, we can begin to fight against God. He can feel like the enemy, rather than a friend.

Profound Suffering

Perhaps the most common cause of doubts is enduring serious suffering. The death of a loved one, serious health problems, financial difficulty, broken relationships—any of these can cause a crisis in the life of a believer. In the midst of such pain, it's easy to wonder whether God is real, whether Christianity actually "works," and whether life has any meaning at all.

Irrational Worry

Some Christians doubt their faith because they doubt just about everything in life! Is this plane going to crash? Am I going to get fired from my job? Are the stories of Jesus really true? For those who struggle with deep-seated anxiety, all these sorts of questions get jumbled together. If they worry about most things, then it is likely that at some point they will also worry about their faith and whether it's really true.

Keep in mind that this sort of irrational worry is not as much an intellectual issue as an emotional one. The doubt is not caused by lack of evidence but exists in spite of very good evidence. I am reminded of a line from C. S. Lewis's *The Screwtape Letters* where the senior demon writes to his nephew Wormwood about how to create doubts in the minds of believers. Realizing that intellectual doubts were not working, Screwtape suggests another course of action: "But there is a sort of attack on the emotions which can still be tried. It turns on making him *feel* . . . that all his religion has been a fantasy."[3]

Of course, there are many other possible causes of doubt beyond those mentioned here. But this is enough to think about for now. The real question is what can be done to address these doubts once we have them.

Facing Our Doubts and Fears

As we have seen, everyone doubts. That is just part of the Christian life. It's not about if but about when. And when it happens, the key is to respond appropriately. Sitting back and doing nothing—hoping our doubts just go away—is not an option. We have to proactively push back against them. Here are a few ways to do it.

Don't Go It Alone

Emma, in your high school years we used to love to watch scary movies together. Everybody loves a fun, creepy tale in which things can jump out at you unexpectedly (well, not everybody!). And as strange as it sounds, that kind of movie can teach us a valuable lesson: it's not good to be alone in the dark. The number one rule for every scary movie—and a rule that is often broken by the main character—is that you don't wander off alone. On the contrary, you are safest when you are with others in the light.

The same is true in the Christian life. When facing doubts and fears, the last thing you want to do is isolate yourself and struggle alone. Sometimes we do that because we don't think others will understand. Or maybe we feel embarrassed that we are questioning our beliefs. But we have to be honest about our struggles and bring them into the light.

Here's where we return to the importance of Christian fellowship on campus (which I brought up in my first letter). You need a deep, strong group of believers on campus who can support you when you walk through tough times. Lean on them. Let them speak truth to you. Let them encourage you to persevere. That's what the body of Christ is for: "Two are better than one, because they have a good reward for their toil. For if they fall, one will lift up his fellow. But woe to him who is alone when he falls and has not another to lift him up!" (Eccles. 4:9–10).

Study Your Faith Deeply

I know that the last thing you want to hear right now is that you need to do more study. You probably think you have enough coursework to occupy your time! But the study I am talking about is even more important. If we are going to battle our doubts, we have to be committed to studying God's word. And I don't mean just studying passages of Scripture (as important as that is), but I mean diving deeply into the entire Christian worldview so that we understand not only what we believe but why we believe it.

If you think back to the discussion above about what causes our doubts, you will realize that each of those causes can be addressed (at least in part) through deep study. If a person has intellectual doubts, studying the evidences and reasons for the faith can help quell her concerns. If a person has lost his way morally, the word of God can be a reminder of the importance of obedience and how God empowers us to follow him. If a person has dealt with great suffering, a deeper understanding of the nature of God—his goodness, his sovereignty, his purposes for evil—can provide great comfort and perspective. And even if a person is a chronic worrier, the Scriptures speak to that too. The psalmist shows us how to trust God with our fears:

> Because you have made the LORD your dwelling place . . .
> no evil shall be allowed to befall you,
> > no plague come near your tent. (Ps. 91:9–10)

Here's the point: *good theology matters.* A believer with a solid theological foundation is able to handle these difficult questions better than a person who has a shallow understanding of the Christian faith. And good theology is not automatic. One must study diligently to attain it.

Get Wise Counsel

Even if you have solid fellowship, and you are committed to deep study of God's word, you still need to lean on Christians who are wiser, older, and more mature. After all, you are not the first Christian in the history of the church to wrestle with these things. Many have gone before you, and you need to learn from them.

Who can provide this wise counsel? Well, one obvious answer is a pastor at your church. Pastors are trained to handle such difficult questions and are therefore a great resource for finding help. Again, this is why being part of a good church is so important. You can also get wise input from a biblical counselor, someone trained to help apply God's word to the issues and problems we all struggle with. And of course, you can look to a mentor, perhaps an older believer who has invested in you and is looking out for you.

Doubt Your Doubts

When we doubt some truth of Christianity, we often don't realize that we are doubting that truth because of some *other belief* we hold. In effect, then, we are swapping out one belief for another. If so, then when we find ourselves doubting one of our Christian beliefs, we can fight back by challenging the belief that replaces it. Timothy Keller provides a helpful example.[4] Imagine you meet an atheist who turns out to be kind, happy, and moral, and this makes you doubt whether Christianity is really true. A little reflection will reveal that there is another belief that is feeding this doubt, namely, the belief that atheists ought to be bad, awful people. And since they're not bad, awful people, then you doubt your faith.

But it is precisely *this* belief, argues Keller, that you should challenge. Why should we think that atheists must be awful people? It turns out that such a belief is highly problematic. The Scriptures teach that even non-Christians can be outwardly kind and good by virtue of being made in the image of God. Moreover, the Scriptures also teach that believers are often serious sinners because we are saved not by works but by grace. So this alternative belief falls apart upon closer scrutiny.

This is what it looks like to doubt your doubts. Fight against the belief that is trying to replace your Christian belief.

Grow from Your Doubts

While our doubts can seem like they're destroying us, don't forget that God may have other purposes for them. As strange as it sounds, there's a certain spiritual depth, and a certain spiritual strength, that we will never reach without going through an intense season of doubting and struggling. When we push through such a season, we can find ourselves all the stronger on the other side of it. Indeed, some of the great saints of old have had to endure such trials so that they may prove more faithful in the end. Even Jesus himself endured a "dark night of the soul." In the garden of Gethsemane, he suffered greatly under the prospect of what lay before him, in anguish even to the point of death (Matt. 26:38).

Of course, in the middle of such doubts, it is not always easy to see what God's ultimate purpose might be. Sometimes we cannot see it until it's all over and we look back. It's worth noting that it was when Martin Luther was in his darkest season of doubting that he wrote his most famous hymn, "A Mighty Fortress Is Our God." And that hymn, born out of a period of doubt and darkness, has strengthened millions of believers since.

———

Doubting can be very painful. It can seem like your entire world is slipping away from you as you struggle through your questions. Just remember, you are not alone. Many, many others have endured this same struggle. There are answers to your questions, and there is a deep fellowship of believers who will walk through it with you.

And God has a purpose for it all: "For those who love God all things work together for good" (Rom. 8:28). And "all things" includes even, and perhaps especially, our doubts.

Love,

Dad

Postscript

What Do I Do If It Feels Like Christianity Just Isn't Working for Me?

The Christian faith is not true because it
works. It works because it is true.
OS GUINNESS

Just one final thing, Emma. The focus of all my letters thus far has been on your *mind*—how to know that what you believe is true. But I want to close by saying a brief word about your *affections*—what you love and enjoy. The reality is that some people stop believing Christianity not so much because they think it's false but because they think it just doesn't work. As they look around, they might begin to think that other groups or ideas or religions just work better. These groups might seem to be rich, deep, and full of life, even offering a better community, a deeper purpose, and a more compelling vision for the world. On top of this, other groups might just seem, well, more fun.

In short, people don't always stop following Christ for in-tellectual reasons. Some people stop because they enjoy other things more than Jesus. To them, Christianity just isn't satisfying anymore.

So how should you deal with this important issue? Here are a few thoughts.

Nothing but the Truth

First, we must remember that Christianity is worthy of our belief not because it always feels better—or even seems to work better than other systems—but because it is *true*. If Jesus is really the Son of God, if he really rose from the dead, if there really is eternal life only through him, then that is enough to make him worthy of following. And that won't change even if the Christian life proves more difficult and more challenging than the other alternatives on the table.

After all, there are some false beliefs and false systems that may, at least for a while, give a greater level of emotional satisfaction than true beliefs and systems. I am reminded of the sci-fi film *The Matrix*, in which the machines have trapped millions of people in a digital dream world so that the machines can live off the bioelectricity produced by their bodies. There is little doubt that the dream world is much more satisfying and fulfilling for these people than the real world would be. Indeed, the latter is harsh, cold, and unpleasant. But the dream world is all a lie. And the theme of the movie is that it is better to know the truth and follow the truth—no matter how unpleasant—than it is to live a lie. In fact, when Neo is deciding to take the red pill or the blue pill, Morpheus is very clear about his promise: "Remember, all I am offering is the truth, nothing more." He knows Neo will wake up to a less pleasant life. But that's okay because the truth is what matters.

Here's the point: we don't follow Christianity merely because it makes us feel good or because it is emotionally satisfying but because it is true. This doesn't mean, of course, that there aren't pragmatic, practical, and even emotional benefits to Christianity. There are many, and we will talk more about these below. But we have to get the order right. As Os Guinness observes, "The Christian faith is not true because it works. It works because it is true."[1]

If we reverse the order and begin to think that truth is determined by whatever works for us, then we will run into some serious problems. For one, such an approach would mean that everyone gets to create his own "truth." After all, people differ—often quite significantly—over what they think "works" for them. For instance, if someone said she found Brazil's Sunrise Valley religion—whose adherents believe they are aliens in human form—to be the most existentially compelling, then we would be forced to conclude that it is "true." Indeed, such an approach would force us to conclude that just about *any* worldview were "true" as long as someone somewhere found that it worked for him.

Beyond this, if we think truth is determined by what is emotionally or pragmatically satisfying, then we will find ourselves always chasing the next great, wonderful thing that comes along—at least for the moment. In such a case, our life would be marked by an endless quest for personal fulfillment, hopping from idea to idea and from religion to religion. Since our emotions and feelings often change, our "truth" would perpetually change along with it.

This problem is particularly acute for Christianity because the Bible teaches that it is a religion that is often accompanied by great sufferings, persecutions, and tribulations. The only way people would stick with Christianity in the midst of such challenges is if they believed it because it was true, not because it always improved their situation. After all, sometimes Christianity doesn't make you feel good. Sometimes Christianity makes life harder, not easier.

Meaningful Meaning

Now that we understand that the truth of Christianity is foundational, we can turn our attention to the fact that it really does provide a satisfying and fulfilling vision for life. In other words, it really does "work." And this should not surprise us. If God is real, and he made all things, then we would expect that following him would lead to a blessed life (as long as we carefully define "blessed").

There is much to be said in this regard, but let me just mention a couple of things about Christianity that make it personally satisfying. First, Christianity is able to provide our lives with real *meaning and purpose*. Of course, everyone craves these things. Humans want to know that they exist for some reason and that all their efforts, labors, and activities are significant in the end. This may be especially true for university students. They want to believe that they are "making a difference" and serving some good end beyond themselves.

But this is precisely where the problem lies. In a world without God, there is no inherent meaning in anything we do. Indeed, many modern scientists and philosophers have admitted as much. Carl Sagan, after reflecting on the vastness of the universe, drew this conclusion, "*We* are the custodians of life's meaning. We would prefer it to be otherwise, of course, but there is no compelling evidence for a cosmic Parent who will care for us and save us from ourselves. It is up to us."[2] In other words, we assign our own meaning to a meaningless universe.

Now, many of your fellow students will resonate with this approach. The world is what we make of it, they might think. So they might come up with a self-declared purpose for their life that makes them feel good. Maybe that purpose is to protect the environment or to fight world hunger or to stop sex trafficking. But does this "make your own meaning" approach really work? Not at all. No matter how passionately one engages these tasks, in the end they make *no sense* in a world without God. And they make absolutely *no difference* in a world without God. After all, why protect the environment? One might answer: To slow pollution. But why slow pollution? To preserve our natural resources. Why should we preserve our resources? To help future generations. What happens if we help future generations? They will live longer, more comfortable lives. And why does that matter? Because . . .

In the end, there's no satisfying secular answer to this question. Without God, there's no reason to think humans matter any more than cockroaches or squirrels. Moreover, everyone we've helped will eventually die in the end anyway. Even if some are slightly happier while alive, we've made no real difference in the grand scope of things. And eventually the sun will die out, the earth will perish, and all our environmental efforts will have been for nothing. Without God, nothing has eternal significance.

In contrast, this is precisely why the Christian worldview is so satisfying. We have a clear purpose: to serve God, glorify him, and build his kingdom. Moreover, helping other people really does matter because they are eternal beings made in God's image and they have dignity and worth. On top of this, everything we do for God has everlasting value because we serve an eternal being who sees all that we do.

Hope in the Midst of Suffering

Another satisfying aspect of the Christian worldview is that it provides *hope when the trials of life come*. And they will come. Now, you and most of your fellow students haven't had to deal with deep suffering yet—that's one advantage of being young. When compared to the rest of the world, most of us have had relatively affluent, peaceful lives.

There is one downside, however, to a pain-free life: there are few opportunities to test whether your worldview has satisfying answers to the questions that suffering raises. How do you face hopelessness? How do you handle loss? What about justice for the wrongs in the world? Make no mistake about it, one of the biggest tests of any system of belief is whether it can provide real hope in the midst of a dark, broken world.

Of course, many secular approaches to life desperately look for hope in the midst of suffering. The problem, however, is that such hope is usually found inside the very world that contains all the suffering. So, for example, people turn to money and creature comforts. Or to sex and alcohol. Or sometimes people just turn to therapy or meditation. And while some temporary relief can be achieved in all these things, there is no permanent solution here to the problem of suffering. For wounds that cut the deepest—abuse, neglect, broken relationships, betrayal, infidelity—these solutions are a mere Band-Aid over the problem.

What is needed, therefore, is a solution to suffering that transcends this broken world. A solution that comes from the *outside*. And this is the promise offered in the Christian worldview. Not only is there a measure of peace and comfort that Christians enjoy now through Christ and the ministry of the Holy Spirit (John 16:33), there is also a deep and profound hope that someday God will set all these things right in eternity. Someday there will be a *new* world, in which the old order of things has passed away and a new order has come.

But what about a universe in which there is no God? What hope would people have? If God doesn't exist, then this life is all there is. Death is the end. There is no making things right. There is no justice for the wicked. There is no accountability for all the wrongs ever done. All that evil and suffering is left forever unaddressed. For those with such an outlook, no wonder hope is hard to come by. No wonder suicide rates are at a thirty-year high.[3] Humans need hope to live, and the secular world does not provide it.

The distinctive hope offered by Christianity explains why Christians have been able to endure incredible suffering throughout the history of the church. Whether it was the martyrs in the early Christian movement or the remarkable stories of people like Louis Zamperini—as told in the book and movie *Unbroken*—who experienced incredible torture at the hands of the Japanese in World War II, Christians persevered because they had an *eternal* hope. As Jesus promised, "In the world you will have tribulation. But take heart; I have overcome the world" (John 16:33).

But What about When Christianity Doesn't Work?

Of course, there's more that could be said about what makes Christianity existentially compelling. We could mention that it provides the power for real change, both personally and in social structures. We could talk about how it offers a wise road map for personal relationships—marriage, parenting, friendships—and how to handle conflict and problems in those relationships. We could explore how Christianity provides real freedom to be who God made us to be, not beholden to the heavy yoke of man-made laws nor forced to conform to the world's ideals. And we could go on and on.

But in the midst of these truths about Christianity, we also have to acknowledge another truth: the Christianity we encounter in the real world doesn't always embody these ideals. Indeed, on the contrary, the Christianity we often encounter falls woefully, and sometimes tragically, short. To be blunt, sometimes the Christianity we see doesn't seem, well, very Christian.

Examples of un-Christian Christianity will not be hard to find in your life, Emma. Some Christians can be mean and cruel. Others can be heartless and uncaring, with no real compassion for the world around them. Some churches can be cliquish, others can be near cultic, and still others are just worldly. There are some pastors who prove to be liars and deceivers. Some cheat on their wife. Others are authoritarian, domineering, and abusive. Indeed, in 2019, the *Houston Chronicle* broke open the story of widespread sexual abuse in the Southern Baptist Convention, spanning twenty years and involving over 380 church leaders.[4] Sadly, we could go on and on.

So what do you do when you are faced with the raw reality of a flawed, fallen Christian experience? There are a few things to keep in mind. First, such problems remind us of why Jesus came in the first place. He didn't come to save perfect people; he came to save sinners—deep, awful sinners. And even after sinners are saved, they don't just become different people overnight. Change by the Spirit is a slow process that takes time. In Romans 7, even the apostle Paul explains how he struggled with the fact that he continued to do what he didn't want to do. His "old self" was still haunting him, and he would often obey it rather than Jesus. But in the end, Paul leaned on the gospel of grace: "Wretched man that I am! Who will deliver me from this body of death? Thanks be to God through Jesus Christ our Lord!" (Rom. 7:24–25).

In other words, Christianity has an explanation for why it doesn't always work. The Christian worldview actually anticipates that

Christians themselves will fail to follow Jesus as they ought. So we should not be surprised when it happens.

Second, we always have to work to distinguish the core values and beliefs of the Christian worldview itself from the way it is lived out by those who profess to follow it. Christianity itself can still be true, even if its adherents make a mess of it. Indeed, we have to make this very distinction in other parts of life. Imagine that I purchase a product and fail to follow the instruction manual about how to use it. This happened when I was in college—we had the crazy idea of trying to wash all our plastic cups by putting them in the washing machine meant for clothes. Needless to say, things didn't turn out well. We were left with a pile of broken plastic shards. But does this mean that there was something wrong with the washing machine? Not at all. If a product doesn't "work" when I misuse it, then I can hardly blame the manufacturer! So it is with the Christian worldview. When things go wrong, the problem isn't Christianity; the problem is us.

Are You Following a Person or an Idea?

We now come to the ultimate reason why we press ahead in the Christian life, even if we encounter a Christian experience that lets us down: *the person of Jesus Christ*. While we will often be disappointed with Christians and the church, we will not be disappointed with Jesus. He is more than enough to satisfy our souls and fill our deepest longings. He is "the heir of all things, through whom also [God] created the world. He is the radiance of the glory of God and the exact imprint of his nature, and he upholds the universe by the word of his power" (Heb. 1:2–3). He is always compassionate, always just, always righteous—the good shepherd who loves his sheep, cares for his sheep, and willingly lays down his life for the sheep.

So here's the key to a fulfilled, blessed life: fix your eyes on Jesus, and make him your great hope and reward. It doesn't mean your life will be perfect. It doesn't guarantee a pain-free existence. But it does mean you can have true joy and peace, even in the midst of trouble. As Jesus promised, "Peace I leave with you; my peace I give to you. . . . Let not your hearts be troubled, neither let them be afraid" (John 14:27).

Here is where many believers miss the point of the Christian life. Some are part of the church because they are excited about being involved in a "good cause" or because they love helping people or because they resonate with the *idea* of Christianity. But in the end, that's not the heart of the faith. We are not Christians so that we can be part of a cause; we are Christians so that we can know a *person*: Jesus Christ. Don't forget, he's a real person, not just a concept. And it is only our affection, our love, our adoration for him as a person that will keep us faithful to the end. If we are concerned only about a cause, that will fade as soon as difficulty and suffering come. Causes come and go. Jesus is forever.

Sadly, this seems to be what happened to Judas. When Mary came to break the perfume jar and pour nard on Jesus—as a way of honoring and worshiping him—Judas wanted nothing to do with it. Instead, the text tells us that he preferred to give the proceeds from selling the perfume to the poor (Mark 14:5). While that was a worthy cause, Judas didn't seem to see Jesus at all. His approach to Jesus was markedly *impersonal*. It was all about the ministry, not about the person. Consequently, when it became clear that Jesus was calling his disciples to a life of suffering, Judas began to look for the exits. For a mere thirty pieces of silver, Judas decided Christianity wasn't for him. Without true affection for Jesus, the cause was not enough.

But Mary was the opposite. She embodies what we should all strive for in our lives—a deep, lavish affection for Jesus. She was not just about a cause. She was about *him*. So real was her affection that she was willing to make an enormous sacrifice, a jar of rare perfume, probably worth a year's wages. In short, she beheld the beauty and greatness of Jesus and realized something. He was worth it.

———

And that's my final message for you, Emma. In the midst of all the challenges and difficulties of life, and even in the midst of competing worldviews that seem to offer more satisfaction and fulfillment, the amazing good news is that Jesus is worth it. He is glorious enough, wonderful enough, worthy enough to spend your entire life on. He is where abundant life is found. As Jesus himself declared, "I came that they may have life and have it abundantly" (John 10:10).

Notes

Introduction

1. David Kinnaman, *You Lost Me: Why Young Christians Are Leaving Church . . . and Rethinking Faith*, with Aly Hawkins (Grand Rapids, MI: Baker, 2011).
2. Cass R. Sunstein, "The Problem with All Those Liberal Professors," *Bloomberg*, September 17, 2018, https://www.bloomberg.com/opinion/articles /2018-09-17/colleges-have-way-too-many-liberal-professors.
3. Sunstein, "All Those Liberal Professors."

Chapter 1

1. J. R. R. Tolkien, *The Fellowship of the Ring*, vol. 1 of *The Lord of the Rings* (London: HarperCollins, 1999), 102.

Chapter 2

1. Cornelius Van Til, *Why I Believe in God* (Philadelphia: Committee on Christian Education, 1936), 12.
2. James N. Anderson, *Why Should I Believe Christianity?* (Fearn, Ross-shire, Scotland: Christian Focus, 2016), 35.
3. C. S. Lewis, *The Magician's Nephew*, vol. 1 of *The Chronicles of Narnia* (New York: Scholastic, 1995), 137.
4. Lewis, *Magician's Nephew*, 136.
5. Frank Newport, "5 Things to Know about Evangelicals in America," Gallup, May 31, 2018, https://news.gallup.com/opinion/polling-matters/235208 /things-know-evangelicals-america.aspx.
6. "Religious Landscape Study," Pew Research Center, accessed July 16, 2020, https://www.pewforum.org/religious-landscape-study/.
7. Greg Lukianoff and Jonathan Haidt, *The Coddling of the American Mind: How Good Intentions and Bad Ideas Are Setting Up a Generation for Failure* (New York: Penguin, 2018), 113.

Chapter 3

1. M. K. Gandhi, *Hind Swaraj, or, Indian Home Rule* (Ahmedabad, India: Navajivan, 1944), 24.
2. Tom Cruise and Oprah Winfrey, "Tom Cruise Asked Hard Questions by Oprah and Preaches," SurvivingScientology, posted December 18, 2014,

YouTube video, 12:48, https://www.youtube.com/watch?v=wN9WoX
K072g.

3. Quoted by James N. Anderson, "Is It Arrogant to Claim to Know God?,"
Analogical Thoughts (blog), May 17, 2015, https://www.proginosko.com
/2015/05/is-it-arrogant-to-claim-to-know-god/.

4. Sri Chinmoy, *Wisdom of Sri Chinmoy* (Delhi: Motilal Banarsidass, 2004), 291.

5. Greg Lukianoff and Jonathan Haidt, *The Coddling of the American Mind:
How Good Intentions and Bad Ideas Are Setting Up a Generation for Failure*
(New York: Penguin, 2018), 99–121.

Chapter 4

1. Donna Freitas, *The End of Sex: How Hookup Culture Is Leaving a Generation Unhappy, Sexually Unfulfilled, and Confused about Intimacy* (New York:
Basic Books, 2013).

2. David Brooks, "The Shame Culture," *New York Times*, March 15, 2016,
https://www.nytimes.com/2016/03/15/opinion/the-shame-culture.html.

3. Samuel James, "We're All Fundamentalists Now," *National Review*, February 1,
2019, https://www.nationalreview.com/2019/02/social-justice-warriors
-conservative-christians-share-moral-instinct/.

4. Back cover of Sam Harris, *The Moral Landscape: How Science Can Determine
Moral Values* (New York: Free Press, 2010).

Chapter 5

1. For more on homosexuality, see Kevin DeYoung, *What Does the Bible Really
Teach about Homosexuality?* (Wheaton, IL: Crossway, 2015).

2. S. Donald Fortson III and Rollin G. Grams, *Unchanging Witness: The Consistent Christian Teaching on Homosexuality in Scripture and Tradition* (Nashville:
B&H Academic, 2016), 141.

Chapter 6

1. Rob Bell, *Love Wins: A Book about Heaven, Hell, and the Fate of Every Person
Who Ever Lived* (San Francisco: HarperOne, 2012), vi.

2. Bell, *Love Wins*, vi.

3. Tim Keller (@timkellernyc), "If your god never disagrees with you, you might
just be worshiping an idealized version of yourself," Twitter, September 12,
2014, 11:00 a.m., https://twitter.com/timkellernyc/status/510458013606
739968.

4. Jonathan Edwards, *Sinners in the Hands of an Angry God* (Phillipsburg, NJ:
P&R, 1992), 17.

5. Miroslav Volf, *Exclusion and Embrace: A Theological Exploration of Identity,
Otherness, and Reconciliation* (Nashville: Abingdon, 1996), 303. Credit goes
to Timothy Keller for my awareness of this quote. *The Reason for God: Belief
in an Age of Skepticism* (New York: Dutton, 2008), 74.

6. As quoted in David Segal, "The Dark Art of 'Breaking Bad,'" *New York Times Magazine*, July 6, 2011, https://www.nytimes.com/2011/07/10/magazine /the-dark-art-of-breaking-bad.html; emphasis mine.

Chapter 7

1. J. R. R. Tolkien, *The Return of the King*, vol. 3 of *The Lord of the Rings* (London: HarperCollins, 1999), 274.
2. To be clear, not all atheists believe in the reality of evil. Some atheists are only pointing out what they believe to be an *internal inconsistency* in the Christian worldview, namely, the belief in evil and the belief in an absolutely good God.
3. C. S. Lewis, *Mere Christianity* (London: Fontana, 1959), 42; emphasis his.
4. Fyodor Dostoevsky, *The Brothers Karamazov* (New York: Farrar, Straus, and Giroux, 1990), 589.

Chapter 8

1. Elaine Howard Ecklund, David R. Johnson, Christopher P. Scheitle, Kirstin R. W. Matthews, and Steven W. Lewis, "Religion among Scientists in International Context: A New Study of Scientists in Eight Regions," *Socius* 2 (2016): 1–9.
2. Richard Dawkins, *The God Delusion* (New York: Houghton Mifflin, 2006), 100–101.
3. As quoted in Ian Sample, "Interview: Stephen Hawking: 'There Is No Heaven; It's a Fairy Story,'" *The Guardian*, May 15, 2011, https://www.the guardian.com/science/2011/may/15/stephen-hawking-interview-there-is -no-heaven.
4. Rebecca McLaughlin, *Confronting Christianity: 12 Hard Questions for the World's Largest Religion* (Wheaton, IL: Crossway, 2019), 111.
5. McLaughlin, *Confronting Christianity*, 117.
6. John Lennox, *Can Science Explain Everything?* (Denmark: Good Book Company, 2019), 17.
7. As cited in Lennox, *Can Science Explain Everything?*, 20.
8. James N. Anderson, "The Laws of Nature and of Nature's God: The Theological Foundations of Modern Science," *Reformed Faith and Practice* 4, no. 1 (2019): 4–16.
9. For more, see Christopher Lee Bolt, *The World in His Hands: A Christian Account of Scientific Law and Its Antithetical Competitors* (Eugene, OR: Wipf and Stock, 2019).
10. Richard Dawkins, "In Short: Nonfiction," *New York Times*, April 9, 1989, sec. 7, p. 34, https://www.nytimes.com/1989/04/09/books/in-short-nonfiction .html.
11. David Klinghoffer, "Yale's Gelernter: To Challenge Darwinism Is to 'Take Your Life in Your Hands,'" *Evolution News and Science Today*, August 5, 2019,

https://evolutionnews.org/2019/08/yales-gelernter-to-challenge-darwinism
-is-to-take-your-life-in-your-hands/.

12. David Gelernter, "Giving Up Darwin," *Claremont Review of Books* (Spring 2019), https://www.claremont.org/crb/article/giving-up-darwin/.

13. For more, see Stephen C. Meyer, *Darwin's Doubt: The Explosive Origin of Animal Life and the Case for Intelligent Design* (New York: HarperOne, 2014).

14. Stephen C. Meyer, "Neo-Darwinism and the Origin of Biological Form and Information," in *Theistic Evolution: A Scientific, Philosophical, and Theological Critique*, ed. J. P. Moreland, Stephen C. Meyer, Christopher Shaw, Ann K. Gauger, and Wayne Grudem (Wheaton, IL: Crossway, 2017), 114.

Chapter 9

1. Craig S. Keener, *Miracles: The Credibility of the New Testament Accounts* (Grand Rapids, MI: Baker Academic, 2011).

2. C. S. Lewis, *Miracles: A Preliminary Study* (New York: Macmillan, 1947), 123.

3. Bart D. Ehrman, *How Jesus Became God: The Exaltation of a Jewish Preacher from Galilee* (New York: HarperOne, 2014), 173; emphasis his.

4. Keener, *Miracles*, 139.

5. C. S. Lewis, *The Lion, the Witch, and the Wardrobe* (New York: Scholastic, 1995), 48.

Chapter 10

1. John M. Frame, *Apologetics to the Glory of God: An Introduction* (Phillipsburg, NJ: P&R, 1994), 38.

2. I credit my friend James Anderson for much of my argument in this section. *Why Should I Believe Christianity?* (Fearn, Ross-shire, Scotland: Christian Focus, 2016), 144–51.

3. Noam Chomsky, *Language and Mind* (New York: Harcourt, Brace, and Jovanovich, 1972), 67.

4. Mark D. Hauser et al., "The Mystery of Language Evolution," *Frontiers in Psychology* 5 (2014), https://doi.org/10.3389/fpsyg.2014.00401.

5. Anderson, *Why Should I Believe Christianity?*, 149–50.

6. Tatian, *Address to the Greeks*, 29; English translation from Alexander Roberts and James Donaldson, eds., *The Ante-Nicene Fathers* (Peabody, MA: Hendrickson, 1885).

7. William Mitchell Ramsay, *The Bearing of Recent Discoveries on the Trustworthiness of the New Testament* (London: Hodder and Stoughton, 1915), 89.

Chapter 11

1. As one example, see Eusebius, *Ecclesiastical History*, 3.39.14–15; English translation from Alexander Roberts and James Donaldson, eds., *The Ante-Nicene Fathers* (Peabody, MA: Hendrickson, 1885).

2. Peter J. Williams, *Can We Trust the Gospels?* (Wheaton, IL: Crossway, 2018), 51–86.
3. Williams, *Can We Trust the Gospels?*, 65. See also Richard Bauckham, *Jesus and the Eyewitnesses: The Gospels as Eyewitness Testimony* (Grand Rapids, MI: Eerdmans, 2006), 67–92.
4. See the discussion of this story in Paul Rhodes Eddy and Gregory A. Boyd, *The Jesus Legend: A Case for the Historical Reliability of the Synoptic Jesus Tradition* (Grand Rapids, MI: Baker Academic, 2007), 424.

Chapter 12

1. Bart D. Ehrman, *Misquoting Jesus: The Story behind Who Changed the Bible and Why* (San Francisco: HarperSanFrancisco, 2005), 89–90.
2. Eldon Jay Epp, "Textual Criticism," in *The New Testament and Its Modern Interpreters*, ed. Eldon Jay Epp and George W. MacRae, The Bible and Its Modern Interpreters 3 (Atlanta: Scholars Press, 1989), 91.
3. Clay Jones, "The Bibliographical Test Updated," *Christian Research Journal* 35, no. 3 (2012): 32–37.
4. Epp, "Textual Criticism," 91.
5. Of course, this doesn't mean late manuscripts are always less reliable. On the contrary, see Gregory R. Lanier, "Dating Myths, Part Two: How Later Manuscripts Can Be Better Manuscripts," in *Myths and Mistakes in New Testament Textual Criticism*, ed. Elijah Hixson and Peter J. Gurry (Downers Grove, IL: IVP Academic, 2019), 110–31.
6. Robert B. Stewart, ed. *The Reliability of the New Testament: Bart D. Ehrman and Daniel B. Wallace in Dialogue* (Minneapolis: Fortress, 2011), 34–35. Dating of manuscripts is complex and debated. Recently, some scholars have suggested that some dates should be later: e.g., Brent Nongbri, "The Use and Abuse of P52: Papyrological Pitfalls in the Dating of the Fourth Gospel," *Harvard Theological Review* 98, no. 1 (2005): 23–48.
7. Ehrman, *Misquoting Jesus*, 211.

Chapter 13

1. Logion 3; English translation from James M. Robinson, ed., *The Nag Hammadi Library: The Definitive Translation of the Gnostic Scriptures Complete in One Volume* (San Francisco: HarperCollins, 1990).
2. There was some dispute over Revelation too, but unlike the other disputed books, this occurred later and for different reasons. For more on that subject, see Michael J. Kruger, "The Reception of the Book of Revelation in the Early Church," in *Book of Seven Seals: The Peculiarity of Revelation, Its Manuscripts, Attestation, and Transmission*, ed. Thomas J. Kraus and Michael Sommer, Wissenschaftliche Untersuchungen zum Neuen Testament 363 (Tübingen: Mohr Siebeck, 2016), 159–74.

3. Irenaeus, *Against Heresies*, 3.11.8; English translation from Alexander Roberts and James Donaldson, eds., *The Ante-Nicene Fathers* (Peabody, MA: Hendrickson, 1885).
4. I credit my friend Chuck Hill with this analogy.
5. For fuller discussion and explanation of what I mean by "apocryphal" writings, see Michael J. Kruger, *Canon Revisited: Establishing the Origins and Authority of the New Testament Books* (Wheaton, IL: Crossway, 2012), 234–39.
6. See discussion in Michael J. Kruger, *The Question of Canon: Challenging the Status Quo in the New Testament Debate* (Downers Grove, IL: IVP Academic, 2013), 168.
7. Muratorian Fragment, 80; English translation from Bruce M. Metzger, *The Canon of the New Testament: Its Origin, Development, and Significance* (Oxford: Clarendon, 1987), 307.
8. Josephus, *Against Apion*, 1.42; English translation from Josephus, *Against Apion*, trans. H. St. J. Thackeray, Loeb Classical Library (Cambridge, MA: Harvard University Press, 2004).
9. Philo, *On the Contemplative Life*, 25; English translation from Philo, *On the Contemplative Life*, trans. F. H. Colson, Loeb Classical Library (Cambridge, MA: Harvard University Press, 1985).

Chapter 14

1. Dimitris J. Kyrtatas, *The Social Structure of Early Christian Communities* (London: Verso, 1987), 78.
2. Rodney Stark, *For the Glory of God: How Monotheism Led to Reformations, Science, Witch-Hunts, and the End of Slavery* (Princeton, NJ: Princeton University Press, 2004).
3. Michael J. Kruger, *Christianity at the Crossroads: How the Second Century Shaped the Future of the Church* (Downers Grove, IL: IVP Academic, 2018), 36.
4. Kruger, *Christianity at the Crossroads*, 36.
5. Minucius Felix, *Octavius*, 8.4; English translation from Minucius Felix, *Octavius*, trans. Gerald H. Rendall, Loeb Classical Library (Cambridge, MA: Harvard University Press, 1977).

Chapter 15

1. Charles H. Spurgeon, *Sermons of the Rev. C. H. Spurgeon: Second Series* (New York: Sheldon and Company, 1859), 303.
2. Os Guinness, *God in the Dark: The Assurance of Faith beyond a Shadow of Doubt* (Wheaton, IL: Crossway, 1996), 24.
3. C. S. Lewis, *The Screwtape Letters* (New York: MacMillan, 1961), 142.
4. Timothy Keller, *Making Sense of God: Finding God in the Modern World* (New York: Penguin, 2018), 39.

Postscript

1. Os Guinness, *God in the Dark: The Assurance of Faith beyond a Shadow of Doubt* (Wheaton, IL: Crossway, 1996), 77.
2. Carl Sagan, in *The Meaning of Life: Reflections in Words and Pictures on Why We Are Here*, ed. David Friend (Boston: Little, Brown, 1991), 73; emphasis his.
3. Sabrina Tavernise, "U.S. Suicide Rate Surges to a 30-Year High," *New York Times*, April 22, 2016, https://www.nytimes.com/2016/04/22/health/us -suicide-rate-surges-to-a-30-year-high.html.
4. Robert Downen, Lise Olsen, and John Tedesco, "Abuse of Faith," *Houston Chronicle*, February 10, 2019, https://www.houstonchronicle.com/news /investigations/article/Southern-Baptist-sexual-abuse-spreads-as-leaders-1358 8038.php.

General Index

Scripture Index